stutter-free speech

A Goal for Therapy

George H. Shames
University of Pittsburgh

Cheri L. Florance
*St. Anthony Hospital
Columbus, Ohio*

Charles E. Merrill Publishing Company
A Bell & Howell Company
Columbus   Toronto   London   Sydney

Published by Charles E. Merrill Publishing Co.
A Bell & Howell Company
Columbus, Ohio   43216

This book was set in Helvetica

Production Editor: Susan Herten

Cover Design Coordination: Will Chenoweth

Library of Congress Catalog Card Number: 79-89649

International Standard Book Number: 0-675-08178-5

Printed in the United States of America

4   5   6   7   8   9   10—85   84   83   82

Foreword

The prospect held forth in this text is at once staggering and iconoclastic. We professionals have all but deified the notion that stuttering in adults cannot be cured. Indeed, for years, we have used claims of cure as a sure mark of the quack. Yet, here are Dr. Shames and Dr. Florance, highly respected scientists and practitioners, reporting that many of their clients no longer stutter or think of themselves as stutterers several years after therapy. How else can this be viewed, practically, than as a cure?

Such a report borders on heresy. Undoubtedly some, perhaps many, will reject outright the prospect they hold forth. Others, however, will probably rise to the challenge of their work and will attempt to replicate it. For such a startling departure from traditional views, nothing short of replication in other clinics by other clinicians will be needed. With such verification accomplished, a new era of hope for those who stutter will have arrived.

William H. Perkins
University of Southern California

*When they hear of it . . . they'll be wild with joy. How much
more there is now to living!
Instead of our drab slogging forth and back . . .
there's a reason to life!
We can lift ourselves out of ignorance,
we can find ourselves as creatures of excellence and
intelligence and skill.
We can be free!*

> Jonathan Livingston Seagull
> *Richard Bach*

What People Say . . .

One client's response to the question, How has this program affected your speech?

Well I recall many times that I had been in restaurants and wanted to order something of my choice and anticipated a block or anticipated stuttering and would select something else from the menu because it was easier to say that word at that moment. And another time I might be ok with ordering that. It was such an uncertain thing and I never knew when I would be all right an hour from now or five minutes from now.

I can recall a specific thing that has happened to me recently. This was two weeks ago when I was in a large meeting of 250 people. And after the speaker had completed his speaking or his speech, people were asked for comments from the audience. And I spoke up and had something to say and said it. And that's the first time in my life I've ever done that.

I used to cross the street to avoid people. I don't do that anymore. And I order what I want to from restaurants. And I have become more efficient at work because I stay in the center of my work wheel, so to speak, and make efficient use of the telephone, which is efficient use of my time. It's a whole new world.

But basically there are things inside of me that have changed, that are the profound elements to me. Without this program, I could never have arrived there.*

---

*This client appears on a videotape that accompanies *Stutter-free Speech: A Goal for Therapy.*

Preface

The idea that stutterers could speak without stuttering is certainly not a new one. We have known for some time that the majority of most stutterers' talking time is free of stuttering. Stutterers have envisioned fluent speech for a long time. However, clinicians have realized stutter-free speech as a formalized goal of therapy only recently. Although we have observed stutterers very closely, described, tallied, and interpreted their behaviors, and agonized over their guilt, embarrassment, and isolation with them, we have historically denied one strident plea from the stutterer: "I want to be free—free from this thing that grips my throat, that twitches my tongue, that makes me shake and sweat and want to dig a hole and crawl in. I want to be free of it—just able to talk like everyone else." It is this plea that this therapy and this book is responsive to.

In a sense, this book is an invitation. We want you to read, to think, and hopefully, to join a growing group of professionals who are trying to deal with the possibility that stutterers can eventually learn to talk without stuttering.

Just as cultures and societies have had their history of four-letter taboo words, so has our professional society had a similar history. One of these taboos has been the concept, as well as the word, cure. The idea of a cure for stuttering has traditionally been rejected by the professionals in the field because as a concept, it has been viewed as anti-therapeutic and leading the stutterer down a path of false hopes and self-deception. More basically, perhaps, it has been rejected because the term cure implies that the cause or causes of stuttering have been identified and eliminated as causative factors and that, therefore, the symptoms will never return. However, to date, the cause of stuttering has not been identified. Therefore, in spite of any therapeutic efforts to modify or control it, traditionalists feel that stuttering in any individual may someday return.

On the other hand, behaviorists have also rejected the term *cure* because it comes out of a medical model rather than a behavioral model of the problem. As a behaviorist, one does not cure behavior. You can strengthen behavior, weaken behavior, control its frequency of occurrence, or help to establish desirable behavior that is incompatible with undesirable behavior. So we still have our four-letter taboo word.

In this book, the term *stutter-free speech* is used. It is not used by accident. It is not synonymous with the term *cure.* This is not merely a game of semantics. We still do not know the cause of stuttering. In fact, searching for the cause of stuttering has proven to be quite unproductive and can lead us away from those concepts and activities that have been productive in clinical management. We do not view the behaviors and beliefs and feelings of stutterers as symptoms. These behaviors, beliefs, and feelings, although related to one another, are manipulable, quite independent of eliminating any underlying etiology of which they are alleged to be symptoms. Stutter-free speech refers just to that—not to a cure, not to its etiology—but to speech that is free of stuttering. This is the goal of the therapy presented here.

This book presents the theoretical underpinnings, the phases of therapy and practical considerations for its use. Part I reviews relevant research, theories, and literature and discusses the operant technology used in the program. It also describes the therapeutic relationship between speech clinician and client as a temporary one designed to aid the client in successfully adapting to his own environment. We draw heavily from the models of the great therapists such as Carl Rogers and others. In Part II of the book, we deal with both the phases of therapy and how to use the program in the public schools. Since many of you work in the schools, we've tried to recommend how to set up its efficient use there. And we've tried to suggest how you could enlist the cooperation of parents.

We've ordered the program into five distinct phases that have proven to meet the needs of clients. Phase I, Volitional Control, allows the client to control his own speech. Its goal is to have the client speak naturally at a controlled rate of speed to achieve continuous phonation—running his words together. The clinician instructs him as to how to achieve through modeling.

In Phase II, Self Reinforcement, the client learns to manage and control his own speech rather than depending upon the clinician for management. The client initiates monitored speech, evaluates his progress and rewards himself with a specified time of unmonitored talking. Thus, he takes even greater control of his speaking pattern.

Phase III, Transfer, focuses on transferring the new speaking skill to the client's own environment. The client draws up a behavioral contract in which he outlines his goals for practicing monitored speech in the natural environment. We use systematic contracting principles to allow environmental transfer and maintenance of natural speaking.

Phase IV, Training in Unmonitored Speech, allows the client to totally replace his conscious, monitored speech with unmonitored speech. At this phase, the clients undergo transformation in self-concept and come to look at themselves as normal speakers. The client comes to speak naturally without monitoring his speech at all. To complete this process, Phase V, Follow-up and Therapy Outcome Studies, looks at the methods we used to collect data on the program's success and shows some sample cases we've encountered.

For each of these phases, we've included a special group therapy for children that adapts the basic program for use with children three to eight. We also have separate recording forms which clinicians may use to administer the program. To show the differences between the basic versus the child therapy program, you'll find summary charts at the end of each phase.

In addition, we've included adaptations for individual variations in each therapy phase in sections entitled "What if My Stutterer. . . . " We've tried to address some real issues encountered in therapy.

It's our fervent hope that our goal for therapy—to produce speech in clients that's free of stuttering—may become your goal as well.

Just as this therapy is intensive, so too were the commitments of the staff who assisted us. The authors wish to acknowledge the contributions of Judith Steele, Janis Shuller, Joan Kaderavek, Paula Rabidoux, and David Domeracki who functioned as therapists for some of the stutterers, as this therapy was being developed and studied. A special acknowledgment is offered to Martha Sullivan for her administrative support which facilitated our efforts. Dr. Florance's participation in this project was partially supported by the Research Career Program, the National Institute of Health, grant #5K07NS00359–02.

Finally, the authors are deeply appreciative to their friends and families for their support and understanding during the time we spent in conceptualizing, studying, and sharing these ideas through the development of this book.

Accompanying Materials

One videotape demonstrating the principles and therapy procedures used in *Stutter-free Speech: A Goal for Therapy* may be previewed by writing to the publisher. It's a brief, yet thorough, introduction to the therapy program from the initial interview through the follow-up procedures with clients. You may request #8099–1 to obtain the videotape in preview from the publisher.

One audio cassette for use with the book *Stutter-free Speech: A Goal for Therapy* simulates the effect of delayed auditory feedback. It demonstrates how speech may be slowed down under five different conditions of delay—250 msec, 200 msec, 150 msec, 100 msec, 50 msec. Your client can listen to a particular rate of talking associated with each of the five DAF levels, and you may reinforce him for matching the sample. Eventually this cassette is faded out because the client comes to produce the appropriate rates independently of the tape. You ony use the cassette in Phase I and Phase II of the program. You may develop your own cassettes for your use with clients, too.

Recording forms are also available to aid you in administering the program to children and adults. You may request #8174-2 to obtain these forms from the publisher.

To order the cassette or recording forms write

Charles E. Merrill Publishing Company
1300 Alum Creek Drive
Columbus, Ohio   43216

Attention: Marilyn Creager

Contents

Introduction

It is indeed a rare occurrence that anyone enters a problem at its beginning and leaves it at its resolution. Certainly, modern-day workers on the problem of stuttering would readily admit that their current work is based on the theoretical thinking, the experimental and clinical research, and the clinical experiences of their predecessors. Probably, the most significant contributor to our current and future knowledge of this problem is the stutterer himself, as he struggles through various experimental paradigms or clinical and therapeutic regimes. His responsiveness, his insights, his tactics and his feelings provide very real guidance. Thus, a partnership has evolved, wherein the stutterer and the professional worker depend on and learn from one another. So it is that books such as this one should be received with a full recognition of the productive thinking of the past and a realization that we as well as others still have much to do. We may be privileged to be in on the final resolution, and for some individual stutterers and clinicians that has been the case. But there is still much that is not understood about this problem and there is still a rich future that certainly is in the hands of others.

This book is a description of a particular regime of stuttering therapy whose goals are to develop speech that is free of stuttering and a self-concept that allows the client to view himself as a normal, non-stuttering speaker. This therapy is not for the clinician who is timid. It requires a commitment to a reality of reaching out for the most of what is possible.

This reality is being shared by a number of stutterers and clinicians who have gone through this therapy together during the past five years. Many of these experiences are illustrated in our videotape, "Stutter-free Speech," in which stutterers themselves demonstrate the therapy and discuss the impact it has had on their lives. Comments like "Talking is fun," "I'm proud of myself," and "I've changed my career goals," are typical of how these former stutterers feel. As one six-year-old little girl simply stated with a smile, "I used to stutter."

There are philosophical, theoretical, and tactical issues involved in the clinical modification of stuttering behavior. A person's change and growth as a speaker is entwined with his growth and change as a total, social being. Such changes may well impinge on his basic self-identity. Questions such as "Who am I? What have I been? How did I get to be this way? and What will I become?" are suggested if not asked. When entering therapy, a client activates a special system of support to help bring about his growth and change. *It is a temporary system*; and our goals as therapists include getting that client into and out of these special therapeutic circumstances and back into his non-special mainstream of society as quickly, as efficiently, and as effectively as possible.

Of necessity, because of the complexities of communication problems, therapy is conceptualized in a multidimensional, interacting framework. Many different things are going on at the same time during therapy. We have the *behavioral tactics* which focus on the specific communication behaviors to be acquired. We have the *therapeutic relationship* which is the context in which these behavioral tactics operate. We have the *client and his will to recover,* his motivation to learn, his coping styles, and his resistances to change. We have the stutterer's *environment* in the form of family and friends who remain interactive with him and may serve to facilitate or to impede his therapeutic regime. Finally, we have you, the *clinician,* as a feeling and reactive participant in the process. The therapy itself is based on the very simple idea of helping the stutterer learn to produce elements of normal speech.

This therapy is strongly based on a great deal of theory and research from the fields of stuttering and behavior psychology. We have tried to selectively translate that theory and research into viable and effective clinical tactics for the problem of stuttering. As a result, we have explored, systematized, and sequenced a number of principles, tactics, and experiences that constitute this particular way of providing therapy for stuttering.

Much of the content of this therapy has come from the stutterers themselves, as they taught us how to help them. Although this book describes a general structure for a program of therapy, its application and tactics are highly individualized as each stutterer moves through his own unique therapeutic experience. Even though many of the tactics and descriptions presented are quite specific and common among a number of the clinical regimes, they provide only *our way of* looking at the processes of therapy and their underlying principles. There is room and flexibility for the individual reactions of the stutterers within the general process. The tactics are constantly undergoing scrutiny and revision in terms of each stutterer's needs.

It is our hope that you will develop those competencies that will enable you to provide and administer this therapy. Hopefully, this means that you will learn *to do* certain things with stutterers for their problems that will be helpful to them. It also means that you will learn to *think about* what you do, and about the ways that stutterers behave, so that you and the stutterer are in a position to problem solve, to revise, to change emphasis, to individualize and to improvise and improve clinical tactics presented. This latter type of competence comes from an understanding of the principles which underly your tactics. Therefore, we will limit our scrutiny of research and theory and clinical reports only to those areas that appear to have direct application to this therapy.

There are essentially five areas of literature which we will briefly cover to provide this theoretical underpinning:

1. Selected aspects of the general principles of operant conditioning
2. Operant-stuttering technology
3. Self-reinforcement and self-regulation
4. Behavioral contracting and environmental transfer
5. General aspects of interviewing and counseling

Not only is stuttering a problem, but also the total experience of therapy, of relating to a clinician, of developing one's self, and of changing can be a problem. The clinician, therefore, is much more than an agent of reinforcement. He is a powerful supporter and significant companion for the stutterer's journey through therapy and change, and ultimately to the termination of this special experience. As a facilitating clinician, your feelings, your actions, your attitudes, your reasoning and judgment, your technical competencies and your commitment are a significant part of this experience. You and the stutterer share the therapeutic experience. You each have different responsibilities and extract different and unique rewards for yourselves. You become partners in one of our most awesome and rewarding experiences; that of combining your mutual talents in helping to realize your full potential as human beings.

Part 1

The Background and Context of the Therapy

Chapter
1

Underlying Principles
and Research

Introduction

The prologue for this therapy was five years of clinical studies, involving a number of short term experiments, revised clinical programming when new ideas about therapy emerged, and long term follow-up evaluations of stuttering clients (Shames and Florance, 1977).

Although some of the tactics and descriptions of therapy presented here are recurring patterns of a process that was employed with a number of stutterers, these specific tactics are constantly undergoing scrutiny and revision. You should develop a comprehension and understanding of the broad issues of the problems being considered so that you too can develop variations in tactics, exercise your own strategic clinical judgments, and employ your own facilitative clinical styles. Beyond our own collaboration, there is a great deal of literature, research and theory that has contributed to the evolution of this program. Although space does not permit a detailed discussion of these works, we wish to highlight and cite those areas that directly relate to this therapy so that readers may pursue them more leisurely and in greater detail.

More specifically, we have drawn from the following areas that relate to this therapy:

1. Operant Conditioning
    Skinner (1953)

2. Operant-Stuttering Technology
    Flanagan, Goldiamond and Azrin (1958)
    Shames and Sherrick (1963)
    Shames and Egolf (1976)
    Siegel (1970)
    Martin and Siegel (1966)
    Curlee and Perkins (1969)
    Perkins (1973a) (1973b)
    Ryan and Van Kirk (1974)

3. Reinforcement Principles and Tactics
    Premack (1965)

4. Self-Regulatory Therapies
    Kanfer and Karoly (1972)
    Mahoney (1972)
    Mahoney et al. (1973)
    Locke et al. (1968)
    Marston (1965)
    Kanfer and Phillips (1966)

5. Self Reinforcement and Self Management
    Bellack and Tillman (1974)
    Rozensky (1974)
    Lefcourt (1966)
    Rotter (1966)

6. Relationship Therapy
   Rogers (1972)
   Rogers and Dymond (1954)
   Strupp (1962) (1972)
   Ivey (1976)

We have tried to provide an overall therapeutic regime within the contexts of:

1. The application of specific behavioral principles and tactics which are designed to change specific speech behaviors.
2. Principles and tactics which address the need to help the stutterer become responsible for managing his own therapy.
3. Issues in the transfer and "carryover" process.
4. A clinical therapeutic relationship as it evolves within the context of interviewing and counseling.

In order to discuss such a series of therapeutic processes we have arbitrarily dissected it into its component parts. However, these components are neither static nor independent; neither parallel nor even sequential. At times, the conditioning processes and the relationship processes are going on in tandem and at times simultaneously. However, our discussion will address each process separately.

Background Research, Theory and Literature Pertinent to This Therapy

Principles of Operant Conditioning

The theoretical perspectives of this therapy's behavioral aspects are conceptualized within Skinner's principles of *operant conditioning.* This system for experimentally manipulating the frequency of behavior characterizes operant behavior as that which does something to an organism's external environment.

The criterion for deciding whether or not behavior is operant is mainly that its properties may be modified by the effects that result from its appearance. In the instance of people and of stutterers we must include the organism itself, not only as an emitter of behavior but also as a part of the environment that provides consequences of behavior. People react to themselves and sometimes modify their behavior through their own reinforcement activities.

Fundamentally, operant conditioning is supposed to stem from a definite pattern of laboratory practices. The subject is trained to behave under certain specified conditions. When the experimenter manipulates these conditions, observations are made of changes in behavior. The events during these controlled observations are categorized into broad classes of stimuli and responses. Some unique relations have been perceived among these classes of stimuli and classes of responses. One such relation is manifest when a given class of responses appears more frequently when followed by a particular set of stimulus classes. *Positive reinforcers* are stimuli which increase the frequency of a class of responses that they follow; their removal reduces the frequency of the response.

Another relation perceived among responses and stimuli which follow them are those stimuli that tend to interrupt or depress responses. This is sometimes referred to as *punishment*. These stimuli are often thought to be aversive since the subject may increase the frequency of those responses that tend to reduce or remove these stimuli.

Negative reinforcement refers to the relation between responses and the termination of ongoing aversive stimuli. Both positive and negative reinforcement imply an increased frequency of responses while *extinction* and punishment imply a weakening of responses.

It has also been observed that certain stimulus events lead to particular responses. Such events do not appear to reinforce behavior; they seem to evoke it. These stimuli come to control responses because they have been discriminated as part of the total stimulus occasion when a response has been reinforced. Skinner has designated these as discriminative stimuli. Thus we have Skinner's basic three-term paradigm of $S^D \rightarrow R \rightarrow Rf$ representing the contingency of discriminative stimulus, response, and reinforcement.

Reinforcement and Therapy

If one views therapy as involving changing a client's behavior, either by strengthening desirable behavior or weakening undesirable behavior, we can see that a clinician plays a critical role in organizing a system of contingencies and reinforcement for those purposes. You can provide the reinforcement, help to arrange for others to provide appropriate reinforcement, establish the occasions for reinforcement, and organize their time, place, form, schedule and source.

Some clinicians have characterized therapy as the *search for the right reinforcer.* We have often had the experience of trying to keep one step ahead of the child and as soon as we have created a motivational game or an enticing reward, the child has become bored or satiated.

With adults, we have often observed that after the initial enthusiasms and changes in speech, many motivational operations such as discussing the need for change, or hopes for the future or approval or tokens may start to lose effectiveness. We then start off on our *search* for an effective reinforcer.

Premack has addressed this problem of finding an effective reinforcer in some of his research and has developed what has come to be

Children receive back-up reinforcers for producing correct target behaviors.

known as the *Premack Principle.* Premack suggests that we ought to use the subject himself as the source of information for identifying effective reinforcers. He states that a subject's high frequency behavior can be used to reinforce his low frequency behavior if we can arrange to make the emission of the high frequency behavior contingent on the emission of the low frequency behavior (Premack, 1965). By observing the behavior of a client, we can tabulate the frequencies of his various behaviors and thereby identify his most frequently emitted behaviors. Our job then is to create a contingency relationship between the low frequency behavior (usually some target response that has been deemed to be desirable and is to be increased in frequency) and the client's high frequency activities (those thought to be highly desired by the client).

Therapy then might be partially viewed as a series of experiences that are designed to change behavior within the purview of reinforcement theory, with the therapist functioning to provide or arrange for reinforcement of the client's behaviors.

Operant Stuttering Technology

Principles and tactics of behavior modification, although ultimately reducible to Skinner's basic paradigm of $S^D \rightarrow R \rightarrow Rf,$ can take many forms and can apply to many theoretical perspectives about therapy in general and about therapy for stuttering in particular. As a result, various operant based programs can appear to be very dissimilar to one another, almost as though each has a totally different base. Therefore, even with their common theoretical base of operant conditioning, different people have focused on different elements of

Skinner's operant paradigm. They have targeted different responses for manipulation, used different forms and types of reinforcement, and arranged different formats, paradigms and conditions for trying to change the stutterer's behaviors.

The operant view of stuttering as behavior, perhaps as nothing more than behavior, was given its greatest and earliest impetus by the experimental work of Flanagan, Goldiamond and Azrin (1958). Not only did they demonstrate that stuttering frequency could be manipulated by its consequences, but that it could be reduced in the laboratory by administering punishment. Probably the most significant aspect of their research was the conclusion that stuttering could be manipulated without direct consideration of the stutterer's anxiety. Up to that time *anxiety* had been a solidly established cornerstone of the stuttering problem. Their research raised questions about this, and in fact cast some doubt about the importance of anxiety in the overall problem.

This early research by Flanagan, Goldiamond and Azrin provided a prototype for some future therapy based on the use of delayed auditory feedback (DAF) and directly influenced the character of Phase 1 of our therapy. Under conditions of such delay, a speaker does not hear himself as he usually does. Instead of an almost simultaneous feedback of hearing oneself talk, there is a slight delay in hearing what has just been said. There is an "echo" effect that typically disrupts the smooth flow of speaking and can result in the speaker being quite disfluent. In the Flanagan et al. research, DAF was thought to be an aversive experience because the stutterers speaking under conditions of such delay learned to slow down their rate of talking as a means of terminating this delayed feedback. Once the new speaking behavior was shaped and strengthened with DAF, this process of negative reinforcement gave way to a process of positive reinforcement whereby the stutterer is given approval for maintaining his newly acquired slow, stutter-free speech.

Based partly on these past views and research projects, clinicians and researchers like Curlee and Perkins (1969), Ryan and Van Kirk (1974), and Shames and Egolf (1976) demonstrated the efficacy of various operant based tactics for managing stuttering. Curlee and Perkins, as well as Ryan, developed their rate control therapies with delayed auditory feedback. Shames and Egolf concentrated on modifying the content of what stutterers talked about and on parent-child interactions as ways of reducing the frequency of stuttering.

It has become obvious that there are a number of ways to modify stuttering or to instate stutter-free speech within the purview of operant conditioning principles. Figure I provides a general, overall model for viewing the paramount issues in therapy for stuttering. It pinpoints these different tactics and processes in the two cells labelled *Establishing the Response,* and *Specific Tactics in Stuttering.*

Ryan (1971), Ryan and Van Kirk (1974), Curlee and Perkins (1969), and Perkins (1973a), (1973b) have developed *rate control* therapies based on the Flanagan et al. prototype. Although they vary in their strategies for employing DAF to establish stutter-free speech, they all reach a similar point in their therapies when they face the issue of environmental transfer and maintenance of the new speech skills. However, these clinical researchers (Perkins and Ryan) have also established slowed down rates of talking, without the DAF machine, by using instructions and examples. By having the stutterer match the clinician's slow rate of talking and gradually increasing the rate of talking to a conversationally acceptable rate, the results are similar to those obtained with DAF.

Shames has used the DAF in ways similar to Ryan and Perkins. In addition, he has used the DAF as a rate calibrator to initially establish a rate of speaking that is quickly strengthened off of the machine, and then returns to the DAF machine for progressively shorter DAF intervals (and associated faster rates of talking). He has also used the DAF as a punisher, wherein the stutterer, once off of the DAF machine, is put back on until he recovers (but for no less than ten seconds) if he "loses" his stutter-free response, inappropriately increases his rate of speaking, or has inappropriate pauses between words (Shames, 1976).

Recognizing that stuttered and non-stuttered speech coexist in the same speaker, some researchers focused their attention on trying to increase the frequency of duration of already existing fluency in stutterers. Fluency, rather than stuttering, was the target response for any contingencies. Both interval and ratio schedules of reinforcement were employed. For example, Rickard and Mundy (1965) shaped the fluency of a nine-year-old stutterer from one and two word utterances to phrases and paragraphs and finally to free conversation. Points and approval were used as positive reinforcers, first by a clinician and then by the stutterer's family.

Leach (1969), paid a 12-year-old stutterer two cents for every minute of talking time. After 15 minutes, he added a penny for every 15 seconds of fluent speech during the last 15 minutes. During 42 such sessions the stutterer's disfluencies were reduced to less than one per minute.

Shaw and Shrum (1972) increased varying lengths of fluency intervals in terms of time for three stuttering children. Different fluency intervals were used on the basis of each child's basal fluency level. Each child selected his own form of positive reinforcer (candy or toy). Two of the children were reinforced for every ten seconds of fluent speech, while one was reinforced for every five seconds of fluency.

In each of these three studies that tried to manipulate already existing fluency, although there were significant reductions of stuttering and significant increases in fluency during the time that the contingencies were operating, these gains were not maintained during follow-up studies.

In a series of short-term research demonstration projects, Shames and his students Kodish, Tucciarone, Witzel, and Schulman employed positive reinforcement and response-cost punishment para-

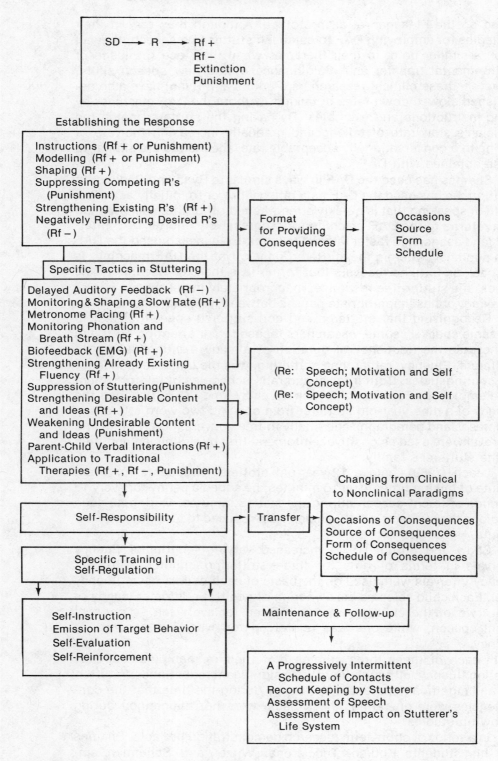

BASIC PARADIGM OF OPERANT CONDITIONING

SD ⟶ R ⟶ Rf +
Rf −
Extinction
Punishment

Establishing the Response

Instructions (Rf + or Punishment)
Modelling (Rf + or Punishment)
Shaping (Rf +)
Suppressing Competing R's
    (Punishment)
Strengthening Existing R's (Rf +)
Negatively Reinforcing Desired R's
    (Rf −)

Format
for Providing
Consequences

Occasions
Source
Form
Schedule

Specific Tactics in Stuttering

Delayed Auditory Feedback (Rf −)
Monitoring & Shaping a Slow Rate (Rf +)
Metronome Pacing (Rf +)
Monitoring Phonation and
    Breath Stream (Rf +)
Biofeedback (EMG) (Rf +)
Strengthening Already Existing
    Fluency (Rf +)
Suppression of Stuttering (Punishment)
Strengthening Desirable Content
    and Ideas (Rf +)
Weakening Undesirable Content
    and Ideas (Punishment)
Parent-Child Verbal Interactions (Rf +)
Application to Traditional
    Therapies (Rf +, Rf −, Punishment)

(Re: Speech; Motivation and Self
        Concept)
(Re: Speech; Motivation and Self
        Concept)

Self-Responsibility

Transfer

Changing from Clinical
to Nonclinical Paradigms

Occasions of Consequences
Source of Consequences
Form of Consequences
Schedule of Consequences

Specific Training in
Self-Regulation

Self-Instruction
Emission of Target Behavior
Self-Evaluation
Self-Reinforcement

Maintenance & Follow-up

A Progressively Intermittent
    Schedule of Contacts
Record Keeping by Stutterer
Assessment of Speech
Assessment of Impact on Stutterer's
    Life System

Figure   1.1   *Operant Model of Tactics in the Management of Stuttering*

digms for gradually increasing the length of time that stutterers spoke fluently during interviews (1973). However, because these were not therapies, follow-up studies of maintenance of fluency were not carried out.

Ryan (1971) and Ryan and Van Kirk (1974) attempted to strengthen already existing fluency and shape both its length and complexity (GILCU—Gradual Increase in Length and Complexity of Utterance). They combined this with positive reinforcement for progressively longer time intervals for fluency and have reported results that are as effective as those programs using DAF.

Some research and therapies have focused on the suppression of stuttering through response-contingent aversive stimulation (punishment). The original Flanagan studies and the follow-up studies by Martin and Siegel amply demonstrated the decremental effects on stuttering of such experimental paradigms in the laboratory.

The research by Martin and Siegel (1966) demonstrated the decremental effects of punishment on stuttering. Their research consistently demonstrated that contingently administered aversive stimulation reduced stuttering in the laboratory. These findings were quite disturbing to the more traditional theorists who felt that punishment generated stuttering. Thus, the validity of two fundamental ideas about stuttering—*anxiety* and *punishment*—were being questioned. However, the research by Brookshire and Eveslage (1969) and by Halvorson (1971) tended to reconcile some of the issues about punishment. These researchers demonstrated that the decremental effects of punishment could be reversed in the laboratory by pairing punishment with positive reinforcement and by preceding contingent aversive stimulation with random aversive stimulation of the same form. In these latter two instances, the researchers presented laboratory analogues of what appears to go on in the homes of young developing stutterers and analogues of those events that may have led traditional theorists to believe that punishment generated stuttering.

Siegel (1970) summarized the results of these studies:

> In the earliest experiments, electric shock was made the consequence of each stuttering; later verbal stimuli such as "wrong" were substituted. In more recent research the punishing stimulus has been a "time-out" period of several seconds in which the stutterer is not allowed to continue talking, or a "response-cost" method in which the stutterer loses points or money for each moment of stuttering. Most of the sessions have been conducted in the same experimental facility, with the subject alone in a room while the experimenter monitors from a control room. In some instances listeners have been added, and the subject has been asked to speak into a telephone. The specific response selected for modification has varied from a global "moment of stuttering" to a more particular behavior, such as a specific facial grimace of a vocal pattern. In general, and with due regard to differences among subjects, all of the techniques used—shock, verbal stimuli, time-out, response-cost— served as response depressants when arranged as a consequence of the response. This has been true with impressive consistency in

both reading or speaking, whether the response was a particular behavior or simply "stuttering." . . . for the most part the results have not been permanent, and subjects quickly recovered their stuttering rates when the stimuli were withdrawn . . . or when they left the experimental facility. This is a familiar problem to speech pathologists. At present a major effort is being made to find ways to move the more fluent speech out of the laboratory and into more natural settings.

The early research of Shames, Egolf and Rhodes (1969) as well as by Shames and his students Johnson (1966) and Honeygosky (1966) concentrated on modifying what stutterers talked about during clinical interviews as the method for reducing overt stuttering behavior. Their idea was that stutterers act on their beliefs about themselves, and what they said and talked about reflected these beliefs. Therefore, they programmed clinicians to reject many ideas commonly held by stutterers that indicated they are helpless victims of their minds and bodies, or that they cannot control their talking behavior. They programmed clinicians to encourage *approach* behavior, to accept statements of insight by the stutterer, and statements that denote decisiveness, goal setting and the expressions of affect and emotion. Their research projects employed various combinations of positive reinforcement (approval by the clinician) and punishment (disapproval by the clinician). They did in fact demonstrate that the content of what stutterers talked about could be changed with conditioning tactics during clinical interviews. They also observed associated changes in the overt frequency of stuttering behavior.

In a follow-up study of these subjects Blind et al. (1972) found that among those stutterers who maintained their gains in fluency, there were significant changes in their life, some over which they had no control (i.e. death in the family, furthering education, births, change in occupations). This was interpreted as an indication that these profound life-style changes gave meaning to their fluent speech and may have functioned in some motivational way for the stutterers to maintain their new speaking behavior.

Still another focus within the operant framework was the research of Shames and Egolf (1971), (1976), and Kasprisin-Burrelli, Egolf and Shames (1972) which dealt with parent-child verbal interactions. This particular research underlies a number of the strategies in Phase III of the child program to be presented. This research hypothesized that stuttering develops in the interpersonal environment of the child; that the verbal interaction between parent and child is a significant factor in the operational contingencies which could be responsible for the acquisition and maintenance of the child's stuttering.

Categories of positive and negative verbal interactions were identified by analyzing videotapes of parents interacting with their stuttering children. The hypothesis was that no matter what the parent was doing if stuttering was observed during the interaction, the parent's behavior could be functioning to reinforce stuttering. The clinician, therefore, was programmed to do the opposite of the parent's behavior during therapy sessions. This *mirror image* therapy resulted in significant reductions in stuttering. Eventually, the parent was introduced into the therapy sessions in an effort to transfer the new speech skills so that they would occur in the presence of the parent and to change the nature of the verbal interaction between the parent and the child.

With still a different focus, Leith and Uhlemann (1970a), (1970b), (1970c), (1972) applied the concepts of the *shaping group* as the vehicle for reducing stuttering and changing interpersonal behaviors. Tactics of operant conditioning were applied in a group situation where the stutterers, as a group, were taught the principles of operant conditioning and were made aware of one another's goals for changing their behaviors. They provided consequences for each other's behaviors and provided feedback about the impact of their behavior on each other. Although results were variable, the concept of a group shaping its own behavior and the intricacies of structuring such an arrangement for stutterers is quite promising.

Related to the shaping group concept is the *Token Economy Approach* of Andrews and Ingham (1971), Andrews (1971), Ingham and Andrews (1971) and Ingham and Winkler (1972) in which a small society of stutterers is established by admitting them as residents in a hospital environment. In this setting stutterers earn tokens for changing their speech. These tokens in turn are traded for certain luxuries in the hospital that would otherwise not be forthcoming. The significance of the research is in their success in arranging for contingencies on an around-the-clock basis. The intensity of the schedule during a three-week hospital stay appears to be extremely important in motivation and in establishing new speech responses.

Self Regulation and Self Reinforcement

As these projects on stuttering were going on, significant research was also going on in the areas of self reinforcement and the self regulatory therapies outside the area of stuttering. Problems in psychotherapy as well as in such specific areas as obesity and smoking had led to the development of theory and technology of self management. Research in these areas dealt generally with developing theory and tactics for self monitoring one's eating or smoking behavior, studying the role of external vs. internal reinforcement, and the efficacy of positive reinforcement vs. punishment. The results of these research projects have a direct bearing on the development of Phase II of our current therapy.

The importance of this research for the problem of stuttering lies in the general idea that as we mature, we should learn to become responsible for ourselves. A very common belief among stutterers is that they are not responsible, but are rather helpless victims of their problem. Although a major focus of our therapy for stuttering is changing the stutterer's speech, this focus should not subordinate the stutterer's needs to manage his life, manage his speech when he is not in a session with a clinician, and progressively need the special support of the clinician less as time goes on. The development of such self responsibility could be crucial to the success of environmental transfer of new speaking behaviors. It does not preclude the usefulness of external support from the environment, but in fact can help the stutterer depend on himself for managing his speech, as well as help him promote positive reactions from the environment for his new behaviors.

Kanfer and Karoly (1972) provide a theoretical model for self reinforcement that involves three stages. The first stage involves monitoring and attending to one's behavior. This tells the person that he has behaved or intends to behave in a certain specified way. In stage two, the person evaluates his behaviors against some agreed upon criterion. The third stage of self reinforcement requires that the person provides consequences for his behavior.

Effective environmental transfer may well require that stutterers systematically learn each of these phases of self reinforcement and that such training should become a regular part of our therapy.

The results of the research on these self regulatory therapies strongly suggest that certain tactics are more effective than others. It appears that monitoring desirable behavior is more effective than monitoring undesirable behavior. In the case of stuttering, this would mean that it would be more effective to concentrate on positively reinforcing stutter-free speech, both in the therapy session and in the environment, rather than tracking, punishing or suppressing stuttering. Bellack, Rozensky and Schwartz (1973), and Rozensky (1973) demonstrated that it is more effective to monitor the intent to behave in a certain way, rather than monitoring after a response is emitted.

Locke et al., (1968) demonstrated that feedback about progress is also an important factor in self management. Although the immediate feedback that comes with prompt reinforcement is important, it appears that giving information about overall progress toward short-term and long-term goals is also an effective tactic.

Motivation in therapy has been a long standing problem and it is no surprise that it has been a problem in the self regulatory therapies. Generally, the research by Kolb, Winter and Berlew (1968), McFall (1970), and McFall and Hammen (1971) have shown that more motivated clients do better. It could well be that the motivation of the client is deeply imbedded in his personality dynamics. But motivation could also be enhanced by the nature of the relationship between the client and the clinician, by the intensity of the therapy schedule, as well as by helping the client to see the possibilities of reaching his goals.

Still another factor in learning to become responsible for one's self is the client's perception of how much control he has over what happens to him. Rotter (1966) developed the concept and measure of *Internal-External Locus of Control.* There is some evidence that clients who see themselves as being in control of their destinies (internal locus of control) may do better in therapy that does not involve a lot of external control; and conversely, the externally oriented clients may falter if thrown into self reinforcement regimes without external support.

Bellack and Tillman (1974), and Rozensky (1974) have researched the measurement and progress of high self reinforcers and low self reinforcers in self management therapy for obesity. It was generally found that high self reinforcers lost more weight in a self control program than low self reinforcers. Rozensky also found that low self reinforcers lost more weight in an externally controlled program.

Interpretations of this research suggest that some people may need external reinforcement, while others may thrive on self reinforcement. It is also felt that *the process of self reinforcement could be learned* and, in fact, in therapy, that it should be given a position of priority as a behavior to be learned that is as important as the original target behavior of speaking that is to be changed. It is also felt that punishment may not be as effective as positive reinforcement in a self regulatory regime.

Transfer of Stutter-Free Speech

The final area of the literature to be considered here deals directly with the format for Phase III of this therapy, *Transfer.*

Transfer (See Figure 1.1, p. 10) refers to that process whereby the client integrates new behaviors, perceptions, skills and feelings into his total non-clinical experience. From a behavioral standpoint he is changing the occasions, the form, the source, and the schedule of reinforcement for his new behaviors. This total integration can be a complicated process. There may be a new identity emerging, an old identity fighting for survival; there may be a mixture of guilt over the past, fear of the future, and a feeling of safety in the status quo. Old and new coping styles and mechanisms may be colliding. This is a time when the validity of the previous phases of therapy is established. It is a time when the stutterer may be quite fragile and vulnerable and in need of strong support from the clinician.

There are many ways to dissect the processes involved in Transfer, and as many ways to sequence the total integrating experience. Transfer should not be viewed as a series of abrupt, discrete, sharply delineated steps. Rather, it is a gradual, fluid process eventually resulting in a change in:

1. Occasions for Rf
2. Source of Rf
3. Form of Rf
4. Schedule of Rf

We feel that environmental transfer, in terms of these four issues, should be initiated after the final form of the response of monitored stutter-free speech is established. Intermediate forms of behavior that are still to be changed are not a target for environmental transfer and integration.

Changing the source and form of reinforcement is a goal of Phase II of the therapy. The form of reinforcement may be changed twice during this phase. During Phase I, if the DAF is used, we have been employing an aversive stimulus in a negative Rf paradigm. Once the stutterer is off of the DAF machine, in Phase II, we are probably using positive Rf, in the form of a clinician's approval for sustaining the new speech response. At this point, both source and form are changed wherein the stutterer learns to reinforce himself with short emissions of unmonitored speech contingent on long emissions of monitored, stutter-free speech.

After the changes in source and form of reinforcement have been firmly established in Phase II we initiate changes in the occasions for reinforcement. This is the goal of Phase III of the therapy. It basically involves emitting the new speech responses in progressively longer units, in more and different social situations, and under a wider array of communicative, linguistic and emotional circumstances.

This could include a systematic consideration of such things as:

1. Size of the audience

2. Specific people

3. Different talking situations (telephone, shopping, etc.)

4. Competition for talking time (being interrupted)

5. Communicative time pressures (being hurried)

6. Topics of conversation

7. Emotional excitement (anger, fear, happiness, loss)

8. Length of utterances

9. Linguistic functions (criticizing, ordering, asking, justifying, negating, explaining, lying, etc.)

10. Interpersonal role

11. Aversive stimulation (being the target for hostility, criticism, verbal abuse, etc.)

12. State of deprivation

As the stutterer approaches this task of integration and transfer, we may need to mobilize as many sources of support as possible to help the stutterer maintain his high level of motivation, keep a focus on his ultimate goals, and confront a portion of his anxiety provoking history and future as a speaker and as a person. We, therefore, seek internal support from the stutterer and external support from the clinician and from significant people in the stutterer's life system.

One format for this process is the use of a *therapy contract.* Although not all stutterers need the structure of a contract, our experience has been that most of them have profited from approaching this phase of their work within this perspective.

Kanfer (1971) states:

> A contract serves two functions in self regulation. The process of negotiating a contract in a therapy program permits clarification of the possible outcomes, their associated requirements and expected consequences, dependent on the person's choice of one of several alternatives. It can serve to motivate a person toward a commitment to change, to establish the supporting contributions he can expect from others, and to make concrete a previously vague interaction or decision to alter one's behavior.

A second function of a contract is to provide a clear statement of specific objectives and the means by which they are achieved. It defines the target behaviors, provides the criterion for self-evaluation, and the basis for self reinforcement contingencies. It is relevant because it specifies *action.*

Much attention has been given to the process of contracting, its functions and its components parts.

Derisi and Butz (1975) point out that effective contracting therapy includes:

1. Selecting behaviors
2. Specifically describing the behaviors under consideration
3. Identifying the rewards for meeting the contract
4. Locating a mediator who can keep track of and give rewards
5. Writing the contract so that everyone understands it
6. Collecting data
7. Trouble shooting the system when difficulties arise
8. Rewriting the contract when appropriate
9. Continuing to trouble shoot, rewrite and monitor the contract until there is improvement
10. Selecting another behavior

They point out that a contract is a way of scheduling rewards between people. It is both a goal and a method. The contract is not imposed upon a person but is negotiated.

When the contract is put on paper, it becomes a public proclamation among those involved. When this occurs, it should indicate the date that the contract begins, ends, or is renegotiated. It should indicate the behaviors targeted for change, the amount and kind of reinforcer to be used, and the schedule for the delivery of reinforcement. The signatures of all involved should be on the contract, including the client, the mediators, the parents, and the clinician. It should contain a schedule for review of progress. It can also contain a bonus clause for sustained or exceptional performance by all who are involved. It should contain a statement of penalties that will be imposed if specified behavior is not performed.

Glick and Kessler (1974), in dealing with contracts in marital therapy, point out that the contract should designate who is involved, the goals, the location of activities, the time, the length and frequency of action, the fee, and the contingencies for absent members and missed appointments. They point out that the contract should be generated by the client and encouraged by the clinician.

Schmidt (1976) points out that contract goals should be established with quantitative values attached to them so that behaviors can be tabulated. This will help make the behaviors more observable and monitorable. The goals should represent a statement from general to specific goals in small steps. He feels that it is more advisable to count an event if it is contracted to be observed 30 times or less daily. If the event is scheduled for more than 30 times daily, it is better to time sample it. For hard to count events it is better to measure the duration of the event rather than just its frequency of occurrence.

He also states that it is possible to provide self consequences as part of a contract in the forms of:

1. Internal self punishment (self verbalizing disapproval)
2. External self punishment (snap with a rubber band)
3. Internal self payoff (self approval)
4. External self payoff (a tangible self reward)

Lathman and Kirschenbaum (1974) apply a growth model to their view of the use of a therapy contract. This implies that each individual, in order to function symptom free, must feel that he is growing, producing and creating in ways that are fitting to him.

The final element to be changed in this process of integration and transfer is the schedule of the contingent activities. Although we have already organized a series of changes in form, source, and occasions for reinforcement of target behavior, throughout we try to maintain the schedule of reinforcement that was used to initially establish the target behavior. The fact that the location and source of Rf has changed does not mean that the schedule has been reduced, or changed from continuous to intermittent, or from a ratio to an interval schedule. The schedule becomes the last variable to be manipulated in the process of integration, and this is the goal of Phase IV of the therapy. Gradually, the stutterer and the clinician replace the stutterer's monitored speech with unmonitored speech. We are seeking a process of generalization whereby the stutterer's monitored and unmonitored speech begin to resemble each other in terms of:

1. stutter free,
2. rate, and
3. continuous phonation.

Sometimes the stutterer generates his own schedule for doing this, but more often the clinician encourages and directs this process until the stutterer reaches a point of unmonitored stutter-free speech. It is in this phase that we see changes in the basic self perceptions stutterers have of themselves as speakers. As they reach that point of doing progressively less about their speech in terms of monitoring, they gradually begin to see themselves less as special speakers, or as special people who are helpless victims of stuttering. It is then that they begin to enjoy the full fruits of their potentials as human beings.

Conclusion

Thus we have reviewed separate technologies developing side by side, one which dealt directly with the operant manipulation of stuttering and the other which dealt with tactics and principles of self reinforcement and therapy contracting. These, in combination with the history and research of *relationship therapy* as illustrated by Rogers, Strupp, and Ivey, are the seeds of the current therapy.

Our goals are:

1. To establish speech that is free of stuttering.
2. To establish a self perception of a speaker that is compatible with his speaking behavior; that is as someone who no longer is a stutterer, or as one who no longer stutters (if that is the fact of his speaking behavior).

To reach these goals *the stutterer learns to deliberately control the rate of his talking* (fast or slow) and *to control how he segments his speech acts,* so that he continuously phonates and continues his airflow between words as he moves forward through his speech acts. Our focus is on the acquisition of these two behaviors:

1. control of rate
2. continuous phonation

The stutterer is then trained to monitor his new speaking skills in a deliberate and scheduled manner, and to expand his speech monitoring into his entire "talking day." Eventually the stutterer replaces his *monitored stutter-free speech* with *unmonitored stutter-free speech.* These processes are systematically scheduled so that he goes through several phases:

Phase I   Replacing stuttering with volitional control over speech (monitored stutter-free speech)

Phase II   Training in independent self monitoring and self reinforcement

Phase III   Transfer and generalization to his non-clinical environment

Phase IV   Replacing monitored speech with unmonitored speech

One of the basic principles underlying this therapy is that the client develops a system of behavioral tactics and rules for strategies that enable him to either move progressively and gradually forward toward stutter-free speech, or if necessary, to back up in a systematic way. A "back-up" system as well as a progressive shaping system is necessary whether we are dealing with the target responses, the occasions and situations, processes of self reinforcement, or the schedule of reinforcement.

As you read through each of the phases of therapy you will readily see how this background of research and writing has influenced the therapy.

Phase I, which deals with developing volitional control over speech, has been directly influenced by the early work involving the use of the DAF machine. In the children's program, Phase I was additionally influenced by the research on parent-child interactions and the shaping group.

Phase II, which deals with self reinforcement and monitoring stutter-free volitional control of speech, evolved from the research on self-regulation, self reinforcement and the concepts of internal and external locus of control, as well as on the Premack principle of reinforcement.

Phase III, which deals with environmental transfer and maintenance, is based on the ideas and tactics of therapy on the contract plan, coming from the areas of family therapy and marital therapy.

Phase IV, which deals with replacing monitored with unmonitored speech, is based partly on the concept of *replacement* of stuttered speech and on processes of generalization.

Throughout the therapy is the influence of the information about schedules of reinforcement derived from operant-laboratory research. Similarly, the content and format of the interviews were influenced by the research on the content of what stutterers talk about and the interviewing and counseling strategies and concepts developed by Rogers, Ivey and Strupp.

We realize that there is a great deal more literature available about stuttering, and a great deal more literature that focuses on operant conditioning and stuttering, and self-regulation and self reinforcement. However, our goal here was not to provide a literature survey, nor to comment on research and literature that indirectly influenced us; it was rather to focus on those matters that bear most directly on this therapy.

Chapter
2

The Therapeutic
Relationship

The Clinical Relationship

The clinical relationship between the stutterer and his clinician is the primary context for behavioral change. At times, other people significant to the stutterer such as parents, teachers, siblings, friends, and other stutterers may be brought into this context, but the basic vehicle for establishing significant and durable changes in the stutterer is the interpersonal, clinical interactions between the two primary participants—the stutterer and the clinician.

The stutterer is more than a laboratory demonstration subject. He is more than a set of push buttons that can abruptly turn on and turn off certain target responses. He is more than an animal running through a maze to reach a reward. As he goes through various phases of behavioral change associated with his problem, he reacts, resists, feels, anticipates, hopes, and dreams. He is suspicious and fearful, and brings his history as a stutterer and as a total person to his therapeutic experience.

In addition to the communication problem of stuttering, the process of therapy and of change can be a problem in and of itself. Changing, even positive change, can be stressful. Recognizing this, clinicians cannot limit their functions to being *discriminative stimuli* (S^D's) or to being *contingent consequences* (CC's) in their attempts to influence the stutterer's behavior. The stutterer needs the human qualities of the clinician as well as her behavioral technological competence. As Fromm-Reichman states about psychotherapy, the patient "needs an experience not an explanation" (Strupp, 1962, p. 582). The clinical relationship starts to evolve with the first contact between the stutterer and the clinician, developing its style and form, functioning as the stutterer moves through the various behavioral phases of his therapy. It is as though two parallel, interacting processes and experiences go on at the same time, one focusing on the behavioral aspects of changing the stutterer's speech and another focusing on such things as feelings, motivation, trust, support, honesty, affection, and respect between the two participants.

We will examine what can happen in this clinical relationship and in turn, relate it to the five phases of therapy that focus on speech. Our hope is to develop a sense of the interactions between the behavioral aspects of the five phases and the processes and attributes of the clinical relationship. Although we are describing what appears to be experiences typical of most stutterers going through therapy, we also are relating material that is highly individualized and sometimes quite atypical. Our comments are based on things that stutterers have told us during therapy, what they talked about as they changed their speech, their interpretations of themselves, and of course, our own interpretations of their comments and behavior.

As the stutterer begins his therapy, his expectations and beliefs about himself, about his problem, about the program of therapy, and about the clinician are the most paramount issues. Many of the initial behavioral tactics and strategies of the clinician focus on these issues. Very often, the stutterer enters therapy believing that he cannot rid himself of his problem, and feels quite helpless and victimized. He believes that there are things going on inside his body or his mind over which he has little control; he thinks that his stuttering happens to him in mysterious and unpredictable ways. These feelings can be so strong that the stutterer may not wish to get his hopes too high. He may not feel that he is worth the effort because of past futilities and because he has become convinced that he is inferior in some very basic fibre of his being. He has a healthy suspicion of therapy and of clinicians. He tracks his failures and weaknesses including stuttering, rather than his strengths and successes. In his own eyes he is a miserable, inadequate, inferior failure as a human being. The possibility of acquiring speech that is free of stuttering and all the social and emotional implications of being free of his problem are too foreign to even consider and examine. Therefore, one of the first and perhaps continuing issues to address during therapy is the stutterer's sense of his own worth and his development of his "will to recover." This does not mean that the clinician necessarily delays behavioral strategies that are designed to change his speech until the stutterer develops a will to recover or develops a feeling that he is worth changing; rather, it means that such behavioral tactics may be exploited for this purpose and actually facilitate the development of such beliefs. Initial changes in speech are relatively easy to accomplish. The tactics for such changes in speech are described later in the book. These early and quick changes in speech can have powerful effects on the stutterer's beliefs and expectations. But the role of the clinician as an interpreter of these experiences is also critical.

Strupp (1972) states, in talking about psychotherapy, that a number of factors operate to make a client susceptible to the influences of a therapist and therefore able to change. He mentions motivation, the current distress of the patient, and early childhood experiences in the forms of defense mechanisms against powerful, loving, judgmental, and trusted parents. He characterizes therapy in part as a patient's struggle against trusting his clinician; and in return, the clinician's tactics are designed to undermine these defenses against trusting her. Strupp further points out that trusting the clinician is a form of submission, a blind faith in the trustworthiness or basic goodness of the other person, and an abiding conviction that the other person will not use the power the patient has been forced to place in her hands against the patient except for therapeutic purposes. Such submission can be painful because it involves risks for the stutterer. The stutterer risks his trust, shares his innermost private feelings, needs, and desires and therefore risks being the target of the clinician's judgments, disapproval, and ultimate rejection. Strupp states that we might think of therapy as a series of lessons in basic trust and that in the final analysis the patient changes out of love for the therapist.

From the beginning of therapy, the therapeutic relationship develops as the client assumes responsibility for content and direction of the sessions.

We have observed stutterers in therapy engaging in the same type of struggle against trusting the clinician, the same type of submission, and the same types of therapeutic bonds of affection. At some stage in therapy, the stutterer starts to believe in the therapy, to trust the clinician, and to submit to the relationship. When we accept a stutterer for therapy to help bring about desirable changes in communication behavior, we also accept the responsibility for generating that person's trust to facilitate those changes. Generating and accepting another person's love and trust is not a casual or unimportant aspect of our work. It goes hand in hand with our behavioral conditioning tactics that focus on the motor aspects of speech. Rogers (1972) has pointed out that the most difficult emotional expressions to facilitate in clients are positive ones of love, affection, and trust. It would seem to follow then, that their rejection and abuse are most devastating to the human spirit. In the clinical context, the violation of a stutterer's trust could be a mortal blow to the clinical relationship and therefore to the entire process of therapy.

Let us now consider how we as clinicians can help establish the kind of clinical relationship that will interact with and facilitate our speech conditioning program. Recognizing the many emotional parameters of a human being in distress, and the individual feelings of each stutterer as he enters and progresses through therapy, we see that as clinicians we have several functions. We are at the same time teachers, reinforcers, models, and counselors. Sometimes we direct by giving instructions or providing examples relative to speech; sometimes we provide reinforcement for certain target responses; and sometimes we strengthen the clinical working relationship as counselors.

The therapy described in this book depends to a large extent on the stutterer talking. It requires that once his stutter-free speech is established, the stutterer can accumulate more and more time and experience with his stutter-free speech in both controlled and protected circumstances, as well as in his non-clinical environments. What does he talk about and to whom does he talk? In the beginning it is to the clinician in a fairly protective and controlled environment. Later, it is in his real world, away from the clinician. Getting the thera-peutic-conditioning process started depends on the ability of the clinician to help the stutterer talk to her. Her skills as an interviewer become paramount in helping the stutterer move through the various phases of therapy.

The clinician as a skilled interviewer therefore addresses two important processes in therapy. One of these is to provide the stut-terer with opportunities to accumulate large amounts of talking time for gaining experience with his new talking skills and stutter-free speech. The second process is, that as a skilled interviewer, she facili-tates the stutterer's trust, love, sense of worth, self understanding, and insight, as well as his personal responsibility for solving his own problems.

The Clinical Interview

Interviews can have many functions, ranging from those that are de-signed to be used by public opinion pollsters, insurance salesmen, employment supervisors, university admissions offices, and medical diagnosticians, to interviews that are psychotherapeutic in nature. Their form and style depend on their purposes. However, unlike our usual social encounters, they have special purposes and a focus.

Most of us think we know how to interview people and most of us engage in it with little or no formal training. This is probably because there is so much overlap between the things we do during normal, everyday, personal conversations with friends and acquaintances and the things we do during an interview. Also, it might be due to the fact that there may be no one right way to interview someone.

For our purposes, we are concentrating on the therapeutic inter-view for stutterers. The special ingredient that differentiates this type of conversation from our typical interpersonal conversations is the *focus.* The focus is on the stutterer. It is the needs, the issues, and the problems of the stutterer that dominate. The stutterer (as he accumu-lates much needed stutter-free talking time) sets the agenda for con-tent and themes, and for what is important to explore at a given moment. We as interviewers focus on him and subordinate ourselves. This is not a mutual exchange or expression of each other's needs. The needs of the clinician are not issues of primary concern unless they interfere with focusing on the stutterer. Our role is to facilitate the stutterer's self explorations and verbal expressions; to help him examine his thoughts and feelings about important issues as he enters into and progresses through therapy. In the beginning, because of his history, he may dwell on his stuttering, and on his historical social and emotional investments in his problem. Or, as he expe-riences stutter-free speech with the clinician, he may examine his fears, doubts, and expectations for the future—his future as a former stutterer. Whatever the content may be, it is established by the stutterer. Our job is to focus on the stutterer, helping him to see that he is the focus and we are there to facilitate his experience.

We have to keep in the forefront of our own thinking that we have been sought out by people who wish to change the way they are. Although these changes are major incursions in a behavioral sense, they may also have significant emotional undercurrents. Changing the way a person is can be profound and awesome and often painful. It is an admission that there is something about himself that is unacceptable. Changing may be tampering with his basic self identity. Although letting go of who he is can involve fear and pain, it can as well involve happiness and positive anticipation about the past and the future. We must recognize that our responsibilities as clinicians go beyond helping to bring about initial changes in motor speech behavior. We are also responsible for helping the stutterer integrate these speech changes within his total self identity. People are more than the way they talk; changing the way a stutterer talks involves more than those things he does with his vocal mechanism.

There are a number of specific and nonspecific interviewing tactics, behaviors and attributes that we wish to discuss as ways that will help you to communicate your genuine concern for the well-being of the stutterer in therapy, and will facilitate the relationship aspects of his therapy. It is through the interview that the stutterer and clinician learn to care about each other. It is also through the interview that they

Table   2.1 *Significant Factors in Clinical Interviewing*

1. Focuses on the client
2. Is accepting and non-judgmental
3. Permits the client to develop the agenda and content
4. Is generally client-centered
5. Attempts to avoid superficial content
6. Does not abruptly or inappropriately change the topic
7. Is fluent and smooth in his wording, phrasing, questioning and making transitions
8. Is relaxed and calm
9. Appears genuinely concerned and empathic
10. Does not interfere with or impede the client's self expression
11. Does not give answers or suggestions
12. Does not deny feelings
13. Can tolerate silence
14. Listens and attends
15. Interview seems to have purpose and direction
16. Respects and prizes the client's dignity and self worth as a person

learn to let go of each other, as the stutterer eventually grows independent of his special therapeutic needs. Just as stuttering is eventually seen as a part of the way he was, so is therapy and his needs for the clinician eventually seen as a part of the way he was.

The attributes listed in Table 2.1 are generally nonspecific. They are not necessarily stated in precise behavioral terms and may require general judgments about their occurrence during an entire interview or a series of interviews. They are thought to be generally facilitating, and are presented here to sensitize the reader to ways of looking at her own interviewing and hopefully to improve her interviewing skills.

Attending

Interviewing is an active process of both listening and talking by all participants. Listening is as active a process as talking. Listening is a part of the clinician's general *attending* behavior that involves both her verbal and nonverbal activity. Being naturally attentive, relaxed, and maintaining good contact (verbally and nonverbally) with the stutterer will permit him to talk comfortably about what he wants, in his own way. The clinician should let this happen without getting in the way or impeding such a process. This close attention from the clinician can communicate several things to the stutterer:

1. If the clinician pays close attention to him, the stutterer and what he has to say are worth attending to and thus respected. Such a perception can enhance the stutterer's feelings of self worth.

2. Such close attending can help the stutterer see the clinician as one who is genuinely concerned about him and that she is really there and available to be of help.

The client and clinician determine behavioral strategies within a clinical interviewing paradigm.

3. By attending, the focus of the sessions begins to take shape and the roles of each participant become more sharply defined. The stutterer begins to develop a sense of his own responsibility, as well as a sense of the clinician's responsibilities during the therapeutic interviews. He will become comfortable with how the clinician accepts him and does not judge him and will begin to take those first risky steps of personal revelation, sharing, and trust.

Besides active listening (silently), attending also involves a verbal following or tracing of what the stutterer is saying so that the content can be accurately stored, retrieved, and reflected back to the stutterer. Comments by the clinician should relate directly to what the stutterer has said to her. Such verbal following can communicate and stress the respect that the clinician has for the stutterer's content, style, and language that characterizes the issues he is considering.

Open Invitation to Talk

During the interview, the clinician can provide the stutterer with *open invitations to talk.* Such invitations give the stutterer a maximal opportunity to talk with minimal influences by the clinician. Usually the invitation is in the form of an instruction, such as:

1. Tell me why you came here today.
2. Tell me about your family.

The invitation can also be in the form of open questions, such as:

1. Why did you come to see me?
2. How did you feel when you stuttered in class?

These open invitations are differentiated from *closed* invitations that limit the stutterer's input for response to very short responses. For example:

Clinician's Stimulus	Stutterer's Response
1. Did you stutter today?	yes, no
2. Do you get embarrassed?	yes, no
3. What's your name?	_____
4. Your address?	_____
5. Do you live at home?	yes, no

These closed structures obviously have their functions during interviews when denial or affirmation are sought, or when specific identifying information is required. They are also valuable when used in combination with open structures. For example:

Clinician's Stimulus	*Stutterer's Response*
1. Are you married? (closed)	yes, no
2. How did you meet your wife? (open)	
3. Do you have any children? (closed)	yes, no
4. Tell me about them. (open)	

Minimal Encouragers to Talk

Like the open invitation to talk, this interviewing tactic also involves *minimal influences* by the clinician. It is usually employed after the stutterer has started talking and is designed to keep him talking, if that is the clinician's wish, without interrupting him. It may be nonverbal, such as a periodic nodding of the head; it may also be verbal, such as saying:

Could you explain that more?
·I see.
I understand.
Hum hm . . .
Yes.
Uh-huh . . .
Silence
Repeat the last few words of the stutterer's comment.
Offer an incomplete phrase for the stutterers to pick up on, e.g., "And then," "And after that," "And then you said . . . "

It should be noted that general attending devices and minimal encouragers to talk can function as positive reinforcers for the stutterer's talkativeness as well as for specific content areas. If such behaviors become too automatic or are used without thought by the clinician, the clinician could easily find herself attending and listening and encouraging material that she feels may not be pertinent to the therapy.

Paraphrasing Content and Reflecting Feelings

Generally speaking, attending, open invitations to talk, and minimal encouragers to talk function to reinforce the stutterer's talkativeness. However, there may be a need to help the stutterer develop a specific focus on content that is directly pertinent to his experiences in therapy. Some things that the stutterer talks about may be more pertinent and more productive to pursue. We are in a position to selectively reinforce these more pertinent aspects. A first step in this process of selection is for the clinician to designate for herself the various forms and classes of content of responses by the client that she may wish to strengthen, maintain, or weaken.

Rogers (1942) has dichotomized clients' responses during interviews as expressions of feelings or as representing intellectualization. Ivey (1976) differentiates feelings from content. We refer to a similar dichotomy of *expressions of feeling* as differentiated from *content that describes the circumstances for those feelings.* For example, in the following statement by a stutterer, "I talk like this all the time now and I'm real proud of myself," there are *feelings of pride* as well as the *circumstances* for those feelings, i.e., the way the stutterer now talks. Our job is to decide whether it is helpful for the stutterer to understand what he is doing, how he feels about what he is doing, and how his various behaviors have been and will be influenced by such understanding. We can paraphrase the content or circumstances for the stutterer's behavior and we can reflect his feelings back to him. Areas of content and feelings that have consistently come up during therapy interviews have dealt with the following:

1. *The quick and easy change in speech*—What it means, its durability, its implications for beliefs of victimization and helplessness, its short term and long term effects; the stutterer's feelings about such change, its meaning relative to being a stutterer, relative to developing stutter free speech; the development of coincidental fluency.

2. *Commitment to an intensive schedule*—The current distress of the stutterer; problems of priority and motivation to change; new expectations and fears associated with stutter-free speech; long standing emotional investments in the problem.

3. *Developing self-monitoring skills of new speech behavior*—Resistance to becoming responsible for himself; fear of giving up the DAF machine; over dependence on the monitoring of the clinician; the dualistic existence of stutter-free speech in the office vs. stuttering outside the office; general implications of self responsibility in areas other than speech.

4. *Environmental transfer of new talking skills*—Conflict and resistance; fear about stutter-free speech in the stutterer's nonclinical environment; gambling on old behavior to see him through; tracking stuttering instead of new behaviors; binding monitoring to expectancy to stutter; seeking fluency and trying to be fluent instead of emitting new speech behaviors.

5. *Replacing monitored speech with unmonitored speech*—Fears of reducing monitoring; juggling the schedule of replacement; maintaining motivation; changes in self perception as a speaker; changing social roles.

Each phase of therapy and those circumstances associated with therapy constitute recurring experiences for the stutterer. They can be areas of concern for the stutterer. The stutterer has different kinds of reactions and feelings to these experiences, and we have mentioned a few that seem to consistently need attention. We may well anticipate their occurrence. Our job as clinical interviewers is to reinforce the stutterer's comments about these issues, to paraphrase his comments, and to reflect his feelings about these experiences so that he can clarify what he is doing and why. We must help him to keep his goals of stutter-free speech and a change in his self perception as a speaker (as a former stutterer if that is the case) in the forefront. Sometimes, a stutterer's progress can be slow; sometimes it can be very rapid. Each of these circumstances can have the effect of reducing the stutterer's motivation for pursuing the final phase of therapy— replacing monitored speech with unmonitored speech. He can become too satisfied too soon and as a result never change his perceptions of himself as a stutterer. Therefore, some of our tactics may be designed to ensure that the stutterer fulfills his potential for progress. By reflecting the stutterer's feelings we can communicate that we understand, that he is not alone, that we are supportive, and that we will help him through whatever obstacles there may be to reaching his goals, as long as he wishes to pursue them.

Other Interviewing Skills

There are three interviewing skills that we will discuss that are quite different from the others mentioned so far. With practice, such skills as listening and attending, open invitations to talk, minimal encouragers, and reflecting feelings and content may become fairly automatic and generally facilitative. However, the tactics of 1) *sharing,* 2) *confrontation,* and 3) *interpretation* are special interviewing behaviors, each for several different reasons. None of these three skills involves the automaticity of the previous behaviors; each requires some forethought (even momentarily) before they can be used. Let us consider each of them separately.

Sharing behavior refers to a tactic whereby the clinican shares something of herself, out of her own experiences of circumstances or feelings that she thinks will facilitate the process for the stutterer. Although we may not share common circumstances for our feelings, most of us have in common a broad array of feelings. Each of us has probably experienced loss, anger, and varying degrees of happiness, fear, and frustration, etc., which puts us in a position to empathize, understand, and perhaps share our feelings, even though the circumstances for these feelings may vary widely. The sharing we do with friends in everyday conversation is quite unlike this clinical sharing. Although we are giving a part of ourselves, the focus is still on the stutterer. In sharing we are not providing a long case history about ourselves, but rather a brief series of statements that may communicate to the stutterer that:

Sharing

1. He may not be unique or alone in his experience. (We should communicate this without minimizing the significance of his experience.)

2. We understand "at the feeling level" what he is talking about.

3. We are willing to reveal to him personal information so that he feels that the trust and risk is mutually shared.

We provide enough information to help the stutterer proceed if he is having difficulty in talking. We give enough to facilitate, but not too much that the focus is lost and his progress is impeded.

Confrontation   Confrontation is a tactic whereby the clinician says something that can be perceived as aversive to the stutterer. Often, a stutterer may contradict himself, show faulty reasoning, or show unproductive coping mechanisms such as projection or denial. As the clinician becomes aware of these types of issues she has to decide whether pointing them out to the stutterer will be helpful to him. Confrontation is a risk because it can jeopardize the relationship if it is really punitive. It may be best to delay confrontations until the clinician feels that her relationship is positive enough and strong enough to tolerate such tactics. Some clinicians feel that timing differentiates a successful clinician from an unsuccessful one. The successful clinician knows when to confront and when not to confront the stutterer. There is an "art of gentle pain" that comes with experience, so that eventually we *know* when a confrontation in a trusting and caring relationship can be effective.

Interpretation   Perhaps the most sophisticated interviewing tactic is that of clinical interpretation. This refers to the process whereby a clinician provides new information or new understandings to the stutterer. Interpretations by the clinician, although valuable, are not nearly as valuable as when the interpretations and understandings are generated by the stutterer himself. As the stutterer moves through his various phases of therapy he may ask for interpretations of what is going on. However, we must give the stutterer every opportunity to reason, understand, develop insight, and interpret for himself. This kind of growth is as important as his changes in speech, and we must be careful not to permit the stutterer to become over dependent on our thinking. There will be times when we will interpret a number of things about the stutterer's problems or about the processes of therapy that are probably helpful. These might involve the following issues:

1. Exploring the stutterer's need to identify the cause of stuttering.
2. Clarifying the sense of control he is gaining over himself.
3. Generally interpreting the course of therapy.
4. Correlating the past to the present.
5. Finding symbolic and latent meanings of what he is talking about.
6. Correlating different current issues in his life.
7. Explaining his coping and defending styles (if the clinician is competent in these areas).

Interpreting to a client implies that we want him to have some new information that we think will be helpful to him. Therefore, it also implies that we have in mind some optimum state of information that he can act on in some way as he reaches out toward his goals. It follows too that we have also implicitly, if not explicitly, arrived at some final goals for the stutterer's therapy. This type of thinking by the clinician is essential and should be explicit, at least to herself if she is to engage in this most sophisticated aspect of therapy. Interpreting means that the clinician is not merely a tape recorder, taking in and reflecting back the stutterer's comments. It means that she is observing, hypothesizing, seeking evidence, and drawing conclusions. In a sense she is combining the scientific method with her human judgment as a clinician.

Throughout these interviews, we are also trying to promote a certain amount of independence and problem solving by the stutterer, so that he can give up his helplessness and learn to manage his problems with less and less intervention by the clinician. We want him to reach that point where eventually he does not need us—for anything. He will know the behaviors he wishes to maintain, he will be able to monitor his speaking when necessary, he will be able to evaluate his actions, and he will generally be responsible for himself to the point where he will not require special, professional support for dealing with the stresses he may encounter in his future. It is within this context of commitment, support, interpretation, and professional companionship—including the tenacity and honesty of the clinician—that the behavioral aspects of this therapy that focus on speech take on their clinical importance.

Conclusion

Throughout this chapter, we have emphasized the relationship between you and your stutterer. It is this relationship that makes the immediate effects of the conditioning tactics durable. The process of therapy and change themselves are stressful, and can constitute problems. The stutterer has a temporary but deep need of you for this period of his life, and there is a special human quality required for this special therapeutic experience.

In our view, the application of behavior modification principles to therapy does not require that we rush helter skelter through our sessions, piling up high frequencies of target responses. Instead we may have to move slowly while the stutterer becomes comfortable and adapts to what is happening. We may have to deal with the stutterer's feelings as he develops new beliefs and understandings and expectations about himself. These sometimes slow, sometimes exciting, verbal meanderings in the stutterer's cognitive and emotional worlds may be the verbal priming for action by the stutterer. As he develops new speech skills and new hopes for himself, he is also developing an abiding trust in our genuine concern for his well being. When we accept the stutterer's faith in us, we also accept the responsibility for helping him to integrate his new behaviors and beliefs into his life, until he no longer needs us.

While thinking about some of the things that go on behind the closed doors of the therapy room, we are reminded of the wistful words of St. Exupery:

> You become responsible . . .
> For what you have tamed.
>
> *The Little Prince*

Part 2

The Five Phases
of Therapy

Chapter
3

The First Session

Introduction

Part II of this book focuses directly on the behavioral tactics that have been arranged into the five phases of this therapy. A separate chapter is devoted to each phase. Within each chapter there is a portion that deals with the structure and tactics of the *basic program* and a portion (when appropriate) that deals with the structure and tactics of the *child program* for youngsters aged three to eight. The basic program was developed and put into operation prior to the child program. It was used with adults and children alike on an individual basis. However, as we became aware of the value of external support and reinforcement from the environment in combination with the self reinforcements provided by the stutterer, a group program for children was developed. The two programs (basic program and child program) are similar in many ways and have the same general goals. However, the use of significant people in the child's environment and the group format are employed as standard procedures in the child program. Groups are used more selectively with adults as their need for external support becomes manifest. Also, there are variations in tactics during each of the phases of therapy that are appropriate to the age of the stutterer.

The first chapter in Part II deals with the first session. Although it is not our intent to guide you through the therapy, session by session, there are special activities and goals for the first session that make it stand out from succeeding clinical sessions. There are a series of very important decisions made during the first session that can influence all that follows.

Each phase of the therapy is discussed as a discrete and separate unit. However, the phases overlap with one another. Even as the stutterer is deciding whether or not to begin therapy he is given an opportunity to experience monitored, stutter-free speech. As his stutter-free speech is being shaped and strengthened in Phase I he is given an opportunity to take responsibility for managing his therapy (the goal of Phase II); even as he goes through his program of environmental transfer in Phase III he begins to replace his deliberate, monitored, stutter-free speech with unmonitored talking (elements of Phase IV). Quite often as he initiates a new level of activity he may be completing a current series of experiences. At times, he may need to strengthen or re-establish more sharply a certain aspect of his behavior that is associated with an earlier phase of his therapeutic regime. The fluidity, pattern, and rate of progression through the various phases of therapy vary with individual stutterers. The greatest individual variations among stutterers seem to occur during Phase III, Environmental Transfer. However, it appears that the longest segment of the therapy is directed toward one of the goals of Phase V: changing the stutterer's perceptions and evaluations of himself from that of a stutterer to that of a non-stutterer, as he finally replaces his monitored stutter-free speech with unmonitored stutter-free speech.

These differing parts of the therapy require continuous commitment and thought by you, and motivation and concentration by the stutterer. There can be no let down of intensity of activity, or coasting, after a goal is achieved. Although the therapy is not necessarily long, nor complicated, nor mysterious, these particular issues vary with each stutterer's problems and response to the therapy. Ideas and thoughts expressed during clinical interviews are converted into action and behavior outside of the clinical sessions.

Our focus in Part II is on specific tactics of behavior modification as they relate directly to helping the stutterer learn to emit new speech behaviors.

However, we should never lose sight of the dynamic aspects of the clinical relationship that breathe life into these tactics and make the stutterer susceptible and willing to participate.

The Basic Program

Before coming to the clinic for the initial appointment, the potential client may have acquired a great deal of knowledge about the treatment program she is about to evaluate. If she has been referred by a speech pathologist, BVR counselor, or another client in therapy she may have been given a great deal of information. On the other hand, she may have merely called the clinic on her own, knowing relatively little about therapy. Most of the adults who come to the clinic have had years of previous therapy. In many of these therapies the client has not reached the goal she has set for herself—stutter-free speech.

Many clients may be very skeptical about any new therapy program. During the initial interview, a number of things must be accomplished; it is most important that the client receive a clear, concrete, and complete understanding of the treatment program so that she may have adequate data upon which she may decide about committing herself to the treatment plan. Thus, the primary goals of the first appointment are:

1. To provide the potential client with a clear understanding of the treatment program.
2. To develop a preliminary evaluation of the nature of the problem.
3. To provide the potential client with an opportunity to enroll in therapy.
4. To schedule the client for subsequent treatment, if appropriate.

Initial Interview

The initial appointment begins with a brief clinician—client interview. In this interview the client is given an opportunity to ask questions and explain the nature of her problem. The client is given the freedom to present the issues she perceives to be important and relevant to her current problem with minimal structure and input from the clinician. During this interview, the clinician attempts to say as little as possible, allowing the client to select the content and direction of his comments. However, the clinician may subtly direct the client's verbalizations toward such topics as how her speech behaviors affect her daily life, her expectations of treatment outcome, her previous therapy experience, and other topics that may be probed for their pertinence. This can usually be accomplished with open-ended questions such as "Why did you come to see me today?"

This initial interview is the only time during the treatment program when the client is permitted to use unplanned, pre-therapy speech behavior with the clinician with no behavioral contingencies in operation. Once the client enrolls in treatment, she will be afforded numerous opportunities to self-explore through the hours of monologue ahead of her. However, during therapy this self-exploration will be accomplished while the client is learning to volitionally control her speech. Contingencies will be in operation to help her acquire speech behaviors that compete with her stuttering even as she examines her problems. These new speech responses have no history of reinforcement. The therapist, clinic staff, and clinical facility can all become discriminative stimuli for this new way of talking with monitored stutter-free speech. Thus, it is important to keep the initial interview and the opportunity for the potential client to use her old speech behavior in the clinic very brief, about a total of 5–10 minutes. The brevity of this old type of speech strengthens the potential for the therapist, the clinic staff, and the facility to function as S^D's for the new speech behavior.

Spontaneous Speech Sample

The initial interview is tape recorded by the clinician. This tape recording provides a 5–10 minute sample of:

1. Pre-treatment spontaneous speech behavior.
2. Pre-intervention self perception of the problem and treatment potential.

During the later intervention portions of the program, change occurs primarily in two areas—speech behavior and self perception. Not only does the client achieve a repertoire of speaking behaviors that are free of stuttering, but in order for the environmental transfer of these new behaviors to be complete, the client should no longer perceive herself as a stutterer and act accordingly. An important part of this change in self perception is a developing sense of control over her speech rather than being a helpless victim who is controlled by her speech. Thus, the initial interview recording provides a record of two groups of behaviors: those related to motor speech activity and those related to self-concept, both of which undergo change during treatment.

The reliability and validity of these pre-therapy samples of speech and self perception are a function of the precision of the method measuring them. The method of measuring phenomena in speaking behavior is a longstanding problem for clinicians and researchers alike. For example, there are a number of ways to measure stuttering:

1. You could count the instances of stuttering over a period of time.

2. You could count the number of words stuttered over the number of words uttered.

3. You could judge the severity of stuttering against some criterion.

4. You could measure the duration in time of an instance of stuttering a) with a stopwatch or, b) with a spectrograph.

The issue becomes what it is you want to measure, what the purpose is of the measure, and how precise the measure should be. Often this issue can be reduced to one of *counting* versus *judging*. Most researchers count and most clinicians judge. There are advantages and disadvantages to each, depending on how they are employed. Counting may provide precision and reliability, but sacrifice validity. Judging may appear more valid but may cause a loss of precision and reliability.

The samples of behavior gathered during this brief, initial interview should be submitted to some form of measurement. Although we lean toward the counting method, the ease of counting, response definitions, and its validity play a big part in whether you choose to count or to judge. For example, in assessing the stutterer's concept of herself from the content of what she says during the interview, we could have great difficulty arriving at a definition of a valid, countable response. We could:

1. Tabulate the frequency of statements about herself that indicate she is a stutterer, helpless, a victim, or without control; divide that by the total number of statements she has made about herself during the interview.

2. Ask a series of questions like:
    a. Are you a stutterer?
    b. Are you in control of your speech?
    c. Do you get afraid when you have to talk?
       and tabulate yes and no answers.

3. Conduct an open-ended, non-directive interview and give the stutterer an opportunity to say things about herself that we would later judge.

We have to insure that whatever measuring procedure we employ, it is replicable, it can be used by others, and its results are not a phenomenon of the person doing the measuring but rather are a function of the behavior being assessed.

Baseline Assessment

Baseline data may serve many functions. They are especially valuable when used to measure behavior change. In this treatment program, existing behaviors are not specifically modified, i.e., the client does not learn to modify her stuttering behaviors or change her current speech behavior in any way. Instead, the client is instructed to produce new target behaviors, behaviors that she most likely has not produced before, behaviors that have no reinforcement history, behaviors that are stutter-free. In this program, the two initial target behaviors are:

1. An exaggerated slow rate of speech.
2. Continuous phonation between words to eliminate inappropriate pauses or breaks between or within words.

Baseline data collection as a pre-intervention measure poses some interesting considerations. One of the primary goals of therapy is the client's ability to produce stutter-free speech. The client does not modify her present speech behavior but instead goes through a gradual shaping procedure to produce new behaviors that eventually replace the previous behavior patterns. Thus, base rate analysis of previous speech behaviors, (duration of stuttering, type of stuttering, number of stuttered words per minute) provide relatively little functional information because there will be no emphasis nor data points about stuttering for comparison as the client progresses. As a matter of experience, tracking stuttering behaviors has been discouraged because it can have a detrimental effect on acquiring the new behavior. When stutterers use instances of stuttering as an S^D for emitting their new behaviors, they have trouble learning the new behaviors, sometimes because of low frequency of stuttering and sometimes because of extreme emotional panic. On the other hand, base rates of behaviors *to be trained* could possibly be taken; however, the initial target behaviors probably do not exist as part of the client's everyday conversational repertoire, nor is the transfer of these initial behaviors a goal or expectation of therapy. Therefore, a measurement of the client's slowed rate and extended phonation of words, phonemes, and syllables also seems unimportant for future comparative uses.

The second group of behaviors to undergo change are those related to self concept. A baseline assessment of the thematic content of her speech attitudes and belief system, outcome expectations, and meaning of change is very valuable. These categories of behavior are probed again and again throughout therapy. From a qualitative standpoint, we feel that the speaker who stuttered only one percent of the time and now no longer stutters nor perceives herself as a stutterer has made more profound change than the stutterer who has reduced her stuttering from 100 percent to two percent but still perceives herself (rightly) as a stutterer.

Vicarious Learning Experience

Following the initial interview, the potential client views a video training tape as a vicarious learning experience.[1] The tape presents clients enrolled in each stage of the treatment program. A narrator explains the goals and rationale of the treatment phase and client and clinician demonstrate the appropriate tactics in a simulated therapy session. Following the presentation of each of the five treatment phases, the section entitled the "impact of change" is included on the tape. In this portion of the tape a number of clients enrolled in Phase III (Environmental Transfer of Training) or beyond explain the impact that therapy has had on their lives. Several clients on the tape explain the initial skepticism they felt when they initially came to the clinic. Others describe some of the embarrassing or seemingly impossible speaking situations that at one time were dreaded and now no longer are a problem. Several clients explain how changing their speech has affected changes in life goals, relationships, and inner most feelings.

Using the video training tape as a vicarious learning experience has been powerfully effective. The potential client is given the opportunity to observe the therapy as the client moves through the entire treatment program. She also is presented with many clients' views about stuttering, this treatment program, and the impact of the speech changes on their lives. More than any other part of the initial appointment, this experience provides a clear, concrete picture of the therapy program and provides an opportunity for a new client to identify herself with the problems and the processes depicted on the tape. It gives the potential client a brief glimpse of what could be her future freedom from stuttering.

The Treatment Program

Following the video tape, the clinician explains the five phases of the treatment program:

1. Establishment of Volitional Control of Speech
2. Establishment of Independent Self Monitoring and Self Reinforcement
3. Transfer of Target Behaviors to the Environment
4. Replacing Monitored with Unmonitored Speech
5. Five Year Follow-up Evaluation of Permanence and Durability of Behavior Change.

If family members accompanied the client, they may be included in the program's explanation and discussion. The client and family or

---

[1]Video Tape—Stutter-Free Speech. A 33 minute video tape that provides an overview of of this therapy is available on a rental or purchase basis from Charles E. Merrill Publishing Company. Columbus, Ohio.

significant other persons are given the opportunity to raise questions about any portion of the treatment program.

Schedule

Scheduling of treatment sessions is the final issue for discussion during the first appointment. Ideally, the client's therapy and resolution of her problems should be the most important activity she encounters. An intensive schedule promotes such a priority. The optimal schedule appears to begin as an intensive one for Phases I and II of the program, while sessions per week are reduced for Phases III, IV and V. Initially, it is best to schedule the client for one or two one-hour sessions per day. The acquisition and establishment of target behaviors requires frequent training sessions for efficient learning. During Phase III, problems of resistance to change, difficulty with adjusting self perception, and assuming self responsibility may arise. If such problems occur, continuing an intensive schedule into Phase III may be necessary in order that steady progress in the transfer of responsibility from clinician to client and to a nonclinical environment develops. However, most often the client is able to master training in the stages of self responsibility (self evaluation, self instruction, self monitoring, and self reinforcement) and transfers her new behaviors environmentally without ambient difficulty. In any case, as the client begins to monitor and reinforce her new speech behaviors appropriately, the in-clinic therapy schedule is gradually reduced while the environmental therapy schedule is increased. During Phase IV of the program, the client is scheduled for once a week; during Phase V, her re-evaluations start on a monthly basis and then decrease to intervals of three months, then six months, and then once a year for five years.

Commitment to Enrolling in the Program

At the end of the initial appointment, the client is given the opportunity to *choose* to enroll in the treatment program. Often adults prefer to enroll for the initial phases during vacation periods so that the highest priority may be made to the therapy program. Children, on the other hand, often feel that any decisions to be made about the therapy program are the responsibility of the parent or therapist. We have found that it is important the children feel the weight of responsibility themselves, from the first session on. Because successful completion of our program relies heavily on the self responsibility and commitment to change on the part of the client, this kind of relationship must be established from the beginning. For many children, this is the first time they have really been given freedom of choice about anything. But through this choice we are able to convey to the child several messages:

1. The child begins to understand that we can show her how to change her speech, but she will need to actively assume responsi-

bility for producing the new behaviors, especially outside the clinic.

2. The therapist does not have a magic medicine that can be swallowed so that stuttering will suddenly disappear.

3. Most importantly, changing a part of oneself is not something "Mom," or the caring therapist can do for the client; in the end the client must choose to change herself.

Although many of these comments have been made with the child in mind, they are applicable to adults as well. Often adult stutterers come to the clinic from social environments in which they interact as social infants. Stutterers may have avoided the activities generally characteristic of adolescent years, such as dating, participation in peer activities, and social and educational group experiences. Many times this results in a very isolated, lonely existence. Thus, the dedication to enroll in a therapy program where the goals are stutter-free speech and a change in self concept to that of a former stutterer can be frightening and threatening. At least the stutterer knows and understands her current existence; most adults have learned to cope sufficiently enough to operate within certain imposed limitations. Changing the entire pattern of a human being's personal contingencies creates enormous uncertainty. For a person who does not fear deprivation of basic needs, uncertainty may be very high on her anxiety hierarchy.

Thus, although it is most often in more subtle and sophisticated ways, the adult may present the same resistance to commitment as those evidenced by the child's behavior. In this first appointment we attempt to eliminate as much uncertainty about content and direction of the treatment procedures, goal expectations, total time in therapy, and degree of time, effort, and money commitment, as possible.

The first appointment is concluded when the stutterer informs the therapist of her decision regarding her involvement in the treatment. She may decide to (a) enroll in the program immediately, (b) enroll in the program when she has more time available, (c) think about enrolling in the program and contact the clinic at a later date, and (d) not enroll in the program. Enrollment on an initially intensive basis is required. By operating in this manner, the decision to enroll in therapy is ultimately made by the stutterer.

The Child Program

The child program is designed for the young child, ages 3–8 approximately. In this program a parent or significant other person is placed in a treatment program in conjunction with the child's program. It is difficult to determine a criterion for when a child is too old for this program. As a child matures and reaches adolescence, she may experience a need for demonstrating her independence from her parents and family. It may be critically important to provide her with an opportunity for personal self exploration and independent problem solving. To place this child in the child stuttering program format could be counter productive. The child might resist changing her speech, symbolizing her resentment of the need for extensive parent training and counseling. On the other hand, the young child may be completely dependent on her parents for her total life experience. Although in the child stuttering program we still attempt to facilitate self actualization and self reinforcement abilities, the child is provided with a well defined external support system that carries her through the transfer portions of treatment. Therefore, a 10 or 11-year-old child may progress more quickly through the basic program using external support systems as described in the adult program. By the time the child is ready to transfer her newly learned behavior to nonclinical environments, the therapist knows the child and family well enough to evaluate the need for external support. Furthermore, throughout the first phases of therapy, the child has been discussing how she will begin to use her new speech outside the clinic. In these dialogues, the child tells the therapist how she plans to involve her parents and significant others in the treatment plan.

Evaluation of the Problem

Three pre-intervention measures are taken for each child:

1. An audio taped therapist-child interview.
2. A video taped parent-child play interaction.
3. An audio taped dinner table conversation.

Shames and Egolf (1976) hypothesized that the consequent behaviors, regardless of form or nature, provided by the parent tended to, reinforce the child's stuttering behavior. In other words, the parent who listened attentively and the parent who interrupted and finished sentences contingent upon the occurrence of stuttering may each reinforce stuttering behavior. This hypothesis was supported when Shames et al. reversed the observed consequent behaviors under experimental conditions and found that stuttering decreased in all cases. Thus, in our pre-intervention assessment we hope to gain information about:

1. How the child feels about her own problem and her desire to change her speech behavior.
2. The contingencies applied to the problem of stuttering behavior by the parent in the clinic.
3. Contingencies applied to the child's talking behavior, the amount of talking produced by the child, and reaction to the semantic content of the child's speech by the family at home.

The Clinician Interview

The parent is given an opportunity to privately explain to the clinician why he brought the child to the clinic and provides any pertinent case history information that may be helpful. The parent then watches the video taped explanation of the stuttering treatment program. At this time the clinician conducts the initial child interview. The child session is usually conducted in a playroom situation where she is given toys or games, as if the clinician were obtaining a free speech sample in a language evaluation. Initially, the clinician establishes rapport with the child and encourages the child to produce spontaneous speech in a free play activity. As the child begins to feel comfortable with the clinician, areas of particular significance are probed. The clinician attempts to learn:

1. The child's perception of her problem.
2. Why the child thinks she came to the clinic.
3. How the child views the environmental reaction to her problem.
4. What the child would like to do to correct her speech difficulties.

Many times it is difficult to obtain a large spontaneous speech sample. The child may be frightened by the new surroundings and strangers, or she may fear exposing her problem and deny that she is aware of any difficulties. Because in this program the child is required to learn self reinforcement procedures, it is important that she independently choose to enroll in therapy. It is only when she is ready to change her own speech that her prognosis for successful completion of the therapy program will be good. The clinician-child interview is tape recorded and, when analyzed, can serve as a baseline example of the child's pre-therapy speech behavior.

The Parent-Child Play Interaction

Video taping the parent and child play interaction is undertaken to help the clinician and family understand the contingencies applied to the child's speech by the family.

The video taping sessions occur during either the first or second session, depending on time constraints. These sessions are submitted to a parent-child verbal analysis utilizing the system developed by Shames and Egolf (1976). This system involves a tabulation of positive and negative thematic statements uttered by the parent. It results in a portrayal of the parent's verbal behavior (positive and negative) as he interacts with his stuttering child. See Chapter 7 for more details of the system, Shames and Egolf (1976).

The Home Speech Sample

A third pre-intervention sample of the child's speech is taken in the home. The purpose of this sample is to provide a picture of the child's communication interaction within her entire family environment. If the family eats dinner together, this is a good time to suggest tape recording the sample. From this tape the parent and clinician gain information about the amount of talking the child produces, the nature of her speech in terms of form and content, the reaction to her thoughts and motor speech behavior from other family members, and so forth. This tape is made after the diagnostic session but before formal therapy begins. The clinician has a baseline recording of the child's speech behavior at home as well as the communication interaction between the family members. This recording, along with the video tape made in the clinic, may become important in the parent counseling portion of therapy. Furthermore, both parent and therapist need to understand the communication parameters in the home as much as possible because the bulk of generalization training will take place there.

Thus, the child's problem is evaluated in a variety of settings with a variety of people. The clinician, child, and significant others are all involved in assisting the evaluation of the current difficulties related to the child's speech behavior in the home, in the clinic with the therapist, and with the parent. These samples of behavior provide the basis for the clinician, child, and parent to work together later in planning and evaluating ways that transfer training from the clinic to the child's nonclinical world.

Explanation of the Treatment Program

The child stuttering program is explained to the parent and to the child independently and as two separate programs. The parent training program and the child therapy program co-exist but interact to help the child complete therapy as efficiently as possible. The child program consists of four of the five phases: Phase I–Training in Volitional Control of Speech, Phase II–Training in Self Responsibility and Self Reinforcement, Phase III–Transfer of Training, and Phase V–Follow-Up Evaluation. Phase IV—Training in the Replacement of Monitored and Unmonitored Speech—is usually not necessary for this age group. Because the parent has seen the film, it is not necessary to provide lengthy explanations of the treatment phases at this time. It is important however, that the therapist explain the purpose and components of the Parent-Training Program. In this program, the parents initially meet as a group to discuss the nature of each child's program, the schedule of daily activities in the home, circumstances that may be reinforcing the child's speech problem, and the parent's feelings and reactions to the child and her speech difficulties. The goals of these group sessions are to help the parents prepare themselves and their home environments for the transfer of training of their child's new speech patterns that will become their responsibility. As the child begins to enter Phase II, each parent will be included in individual sessions with his child so that he will learn the self reinforcement paradigm as it applies to his child personally. Then the parent, child, and therapist will work together to design the transfer of training program. Thus, during this portion of the child diagnostic session, the parent is given a brief explanation of the child's stuttering treatment program and the parent training program.

Schedule

The schedule for the child stuttering program follows the basic pattern of the adult program. The child attends a one-hour group session daily for Phases I and II with a progressive reduction in scheduled clinic visits as the home therapy program expands during Phase III. Unlike the adult program, the children are seen in small groups during the clinic program. During Phases I and II the parent attends the parent training-counseling group sessions and becomes part of direct therapy as the child begins Phase III.

Enrolling in Treatment

A child is eligible to enroll in our treatment program if she meets the following criteria:

1. She must independently choose to enroll in therapy. Her parents or teacher cannot make the decision.
2. She or her family present concern about her speech behavior.
3. She and her parent must commit themselves to adequate time for therapy.

Chapter
4

Phase I Volitional Control

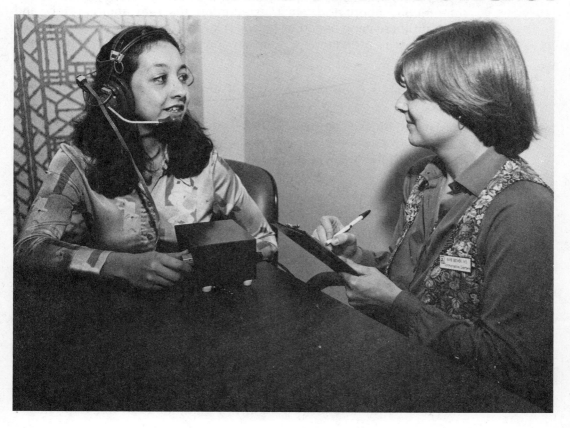

The Basic Program

During Phase I the client is trained to produce elements characteristic of normal speech. These elements compete with stuttering behavior and result in stutter-free speech. The training paradigm begins by instructing the subject to produce a very slow rate of speech, stretching each word into the following word to produce continuous phonation throughout the speech act and to eliminate pauses or interruptions that disrupt spontaneous conversational speech. To effectively train a consistent slow rate of speech, we utilize a delayed auditory feedback signal (250 milliseconds). By slowing the linguistic and motoric encoding process down to an abnormal rate, the client gives himself time to concentrate on producing the target behavior: continuous phonation. He must control his rate appropriately and without increasing speed or he will hear the delayed speech signal as a negative reinforcer. The goals of the first phase of the treatment program are:

1. To establish volitional control of continuous phonation, rate and prosody.
2. To establish a normal response in terms of the suprasegmental aspects of speech.
3. To establish speech that is free of stuttering.

The Treatment Paradigm

The client is required to complete 30 minutes of stutter-free speech at each of five delay intervals on the DAF machine (250, 200, 150, 100 and 50 msec.). Initially, a period of training is necessary to teach the correct response on DAF. The client is instructed to slow down his speech until he no longer hears the echo through the earphones or until it sounds as if the two voices are speaking at the same rate. If the client appears to need further explanation, the clinician can show the client the tape loop and explain that the DAF is simply a tape recorder that plays the client's speech back at a specific rate of delay. The major objective for the client is to slow his speech down until the speech on the tape loop and his on-line verbalizations are at the same rate and he is no longer aware of any delay through the earphones.

The Initial Response

When therapy begins, the client is required to speak under conditions of 250 msec. delay. A correct response is one that is slow enough so that the speaker does not hear the delayed feedback and one in which continuous phonation is produced between words. The clinician may ask the client to model short sentences and then ask the client to evaluate continuous phonation and rate. Once the client understands how to self-monitor these two aspects of the response, the clinician allows the client to continue talking until 30 minutes of stutter-free speech, in which appropriate rate, prosody and continuous phonation are maintained.

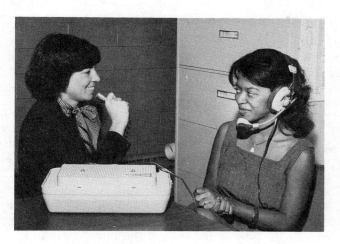

The client is trained to produce elements of normal speech under conditions of delayed auditory feedback.

If the client experiences difficulty producing the target response, the clinician may utilize any of the following back-up procedures to simplify the task.

1. *Reading* The client may find it easier to concentrate on monitoring rate and continuous phonation when reading. Generally, oral reading is an easier task than talking due to the absence of programming semantic intentions. In other words, the client does not need to program his thoughts and ideas into expressive language units, he merely reads from the printed page.

2. *Automatic Speech* Some clients have a poor reinforcement history associated with oral reading, and fear such a task. Thus, in this case another way of simplifying the task is to ask the client to produce automatic speech such as counting or days of the week. Again the semantic intent of the verbalization has been removed and the client may find it easier to concentrate on the target responses and evaluate his production.

3. *Stretching the Phonemes* In rare instances the client will experience difficulty running words together. He will pause between or within words when asked to do any of the above tasks. This behavior is a characteristic of his old speech response that needs to be replaced by continuous phonation. In this case, the clinician may need to break the response down to the phoneme level. The client

is then required to stretch out and prolong each phoneme in a sequence, dragging one phoneme into the next, so that he may begin to feel the overlapping ballistic movements of co-articulation. In this way the client begins to develop a motor-kinesthetic awareness of the elements of continuous phonation. He begins to sense his own ability to volitionally control various components of the motor speech act.

4. *Word Groups*   Once the client is able to produce phonemes in a continuous string, the clinician instructs the client to produce and evaluate one-word units, two-word units, three-word units until he is able to read simple sentences, paragraphs with appropriate phrasing, and can finally produce speech with communicative intent.

Increasing Rate of Response

Once the client learns to produce, monitor, and evaluate the target behaviors, continuous phonation, and volitional control of rate in conversational speech, he is required to complete 30 minutes of stutter-free speech at each of five delay levels (250, 200, 150, 100, 50 msec. delay). As the delay time is decreased the client is able to produce a faster speech rate without hearing the delayed feedback through the earphones. Thus, as the delay is decreased the client begins to increase his own rate of speech, gradually approaching a normal speech rate. At the 250 msec. rate, the client's speech is so abnormally slow that it is difficult to monitor and evaluate the suprasegmental aspects of his response. Once he begins to increase his rate however, (150–50 msec. delay) difficulties in prosody and speech affect may be noted and given attention. For example, the client may utilize monopitch and monoloudness, avoiding normal inflections and stress, or he may begin to speak with a metronomic effect, producing a speech response with a consistent isocranous beat at equal appearing intervals. These types of speech behaviors contribute to an overall response that may be stutter-free, but the robot-like speech that results is highly undesirable and draws attention to itself. These types of off-target variations of the correct response can be easily extinguished if they are attended to early in the training period. At the very slow rates it is often difficult to evaluate good speech prosody and appropriate inflection and phrasing. It is not too early, however, to eliminate monopitch, monoloudness, or metronome effect. If these off-target responses are highlighted immediately and the client is taught to model correct speech inflection and stress, further problems usually do not arise. However, if left unattended, the client begins to accept these behaviors as an integral part of the new speech response he is learning and they can become strongly conditioned and difficult to extinguish.

Secondary Behaviors

As the client begins to volitionally program the components of the new stutter-free speech response, any overt secondary behaviors such as head jerks, tics, eye blinks, and so forth, have generally disappeared on-line. However, a stutterer may have covert strategies of circumlocuting or substituting words. It is important that the clinician explain to the client that he is learning a totally new speech response and that in order for this to completely replace his old speech behavior, it is necessary to completely eliminate all of his old habits. Therefore, if he catches himself anticipating or fearing specific words, he should immediately bring this to the attention of the clinician. The clinician can then make sure that the client is focused on instructing the motoric programming system to produce continuous phonation and appropriate rate, rather than the off-target behaviors he may have produced in a similar situation in the past.

Eye contact may also be a problem. The client should be instructed to maintain appropriate eye contact if he is not doing so as early in the treatment program as possible. If the problem persists, the client may be asked to look at the clinician and several other specific objects in the room, until his old off-target, undesirable behavior is replaced by appropriate ones.

Contingencies for Off-Target Behavior

Any off-target behavior including stuttering, avoiding words, inappropriate pausing, and inappropriate rate must be extinguished so that a solid and correct new motor speech response is instated. If the client produces any of the above behaviors while accumulating the 30 minutes at one of the delay levels, a contingency is imposed. This contingency requires the client to remain at that delay level for an additional five-minute period before advancing to the next level.

Communicative Content

Basically, for roughly a three-hour period of motor-speech training the client will be learning to volitionally control certain aspects of his speech that are incompatible with stuttering. During this training period, it is important for the client to produce continuous conversational speech in more or less a monologue fashion. This program is designed not only to teach a new motor speech response but also to facilitate the personal growth and problem-solving abilities of the client. In this way the client will be able to leave his old speech behind and make changes in his life system in concert with his newly acquired normal speech. Thus, it is important for the clinician to be as non-directive as possible in regard to the selection of conversational topics for the therapy sessions. The client needs to feel the responsibility of organizing the direction of the sessions so that he talks about areas he feels concerned about and that he decides are important for exploration as part of the clinical process. Sometimes the client may have initial difficulty in determining topics of conversation for a full hour period. In this case, the client might be asked to select several topics for discussion at the beginning of the session. The clinician can then utilize her interviewing skills to increase verbal output while the client's integrity in terms of controlling the direction of the session is maintained. As the client–clinician relationship matures, problems regarding the content for discussion within the session usually diminish.

Volitional Control of the Motor Speech Response

It is important for the client to realize that he is producing this new speech response rather than feeling that the DAF machine is controlling his speech mechanism. Typically, the stutterer feels that he is the helpless victim of his speech disorder. He does not know what caused his problem and many times—even with years of therapy—he has not succeeded in remediating the problem. As a result he feels that stuttering is something that through no fault of his own has happened to him, a circumstance that cannot be changed. Therefore, for many clients it is extremely difficult to accept the notion of volitional control of the motor speech mechanism. In the past the client may have desired to produce one behavior and many other undesirable behaviors seemed to occur unexpectedly. Often it is much easier for the client to believe that the DAF machine changes his speech rather than the fact that he is beginning to assume control of his speech musculature. Thus, it is a good idea for the client to replicate his new speech responses off the machine, even as early as the 250 msec. phase. As he begins to realize that he can produce the correct target responses off the machine, he begins to understand that the machine is just a source of feedback to provide contingencies for controlling his rate. The client begins to see himself, then, as the primary agent of behavior change.

To strengthen the stutterer's sense of controlling his speech behavior after he reaches the 30 minute stutter-free criterion at each DAF level, the DAF machine is turned off (the earphones are still on the stutterer), and the stutterer is asked to speak as though the DAF machine were still on at that particular DAF interval. He is asked to maintain the same slowed down rate and continuous phonation style of talking for a period of two to three minutes; he is questioned during this time about his feeling of control over his speech.

Toward the end of Phase I, after the stutterer has met the 30 minute criterion for all of the DAF intervals, he is given the experience of abruptly changing the rate of his speech. This is accomplished by the clinician abruptly changing the DAF levels back and forth from 50 msec. to 250 msec., giving the stutterer about 30 seconds of talking time at each level. This is done for about five minutes. Eventually the stutterer operates the DAF machine and manages his own abrupt changes in DAF levels and accompanying changes in rate. This step in the therapy strengthens the stutterer's sense of control over his speech, gets him more deeply involved in self management operations, and sets the stage for his experiences in Part II of the therapy: the development of self responsibility and self reinforcement tactics.

Date	Condition	Crit. Time	Acc. Crit. Time	Acc. Non Crit. Time	Date	Condition	Crit. Time	Acc. Crit. Time	Acc. Non Crit. Time

Figure 4.1 *Phase 1 Data Record*

Alternatives for Training the Speech Responses

For adults, the use of the DAF machine appears to be the fastest way to establish monitored stutter-free speech. The negative reinforcement paradigm is prompt, the stutterer gets immediate consequences for emitting his slowed down speech, the termination of the aversive delayed speech signal.

However, we have found other simple ways of achieving the same results. These have been quite effective with adults, and are preferred for young children.

Stutterers have been given an example by the clinician of slowed down speech and of continuous phonation and asked to imitate the model.

Another strategy has been to put the stutterer on the DAF machine for a very short period of time until he has acquired the rate appropriate for each of the five DAF levels, and then have him complete the 30 minute criterion while talking off the machine. In this program, he goes back to the machine each time he completes the criterion for a specific DAF level in order to calibrate his rate for the next DAF level. He also goes back to the machine for a minimum of 10 seconds of talking or until he regains the appropriate speech response if he:

1. Stutters

2. Speaks with an inappropriately fast rate.

3. Fragments his speech with pauses between words.

The Child Program

Essentially, the goals and principles of the basic program are the same for the child program. The tactics, however, have been changed so that communicative interactions are suited to the child's needs. In the basic program the client engages in therapeutic monologues while the clinician listens, attends, and through his interviewing skills encourages independent problem-solving behavior. For the young child, the one-hour daily monologue session is inappropriate, if not impossible. Therefore, we enroll them in small groups of three or four close to one another in age. In this way they can communicate with each other as well as with the adult therapist; this more closely parallels the kind of communicative interactions the child experiences in the real world. Further, although the young child may have developed some negative feelings about himself, he has not accumulated the long term reinforcement history that the adult has. As a result, we have found that in most cases it is generally easier for the child to undergo the change process than it is for adults. Their need for an intensive relationship with an adult therapist is different from the adult stutterer's needs for this type of relationship.

The Treatment Paradigm

Each child in the group is required to complete 15 minutes of stutter-free speech at each of the five levels on the DAF machine. The therapist engages the children in communicative activity by using open-ended invitations to talk or questions such as "Tell me about your favorite TV show." or "Tell me about your favorite game." She may use language stimulation cards, sequence pictures, puppets, or chain stories. The children take turns practicing their new speech behaviors. Each child takes a turn sitting in the special *smooth speech chair,* where he produces the target behaviors of slow rate and continuous phonation under conditions of DAF. Initially the child receives a tangible reinforcer for each two words produced correctly. As long as he continues to produce stutter-free speech, the child can continue talking and thereby earn more reinforcers or points until he accumulates a total of five minutes of good speech. When he achieves his five minute criterion level or if he produces off-target behavior any time during the five minute period, he records the accumulated points and relinquishes the chair to the next child. Thus, although a total of 15 minutes is needed for each rate, the child accumulates his stutter-free speech time in five minute blocks. In this way the children take turns more frequently, yielding a more closely simulated conversational situation, and the therapist can use comments from one child to stimulate spontaneous speech from another. The children not sitting in the smooth speech chair are either listening to the "speaker," timing him, evaluating him, or reinforcing him with chips. As members of the group they may be vicariously experiencing the process and thereby are facilitated in their respective turns in the speech chair.

Reinforcement Schedule

The reinforcement schedule begins with one reinforcer given for each correctly produced two-word unit. This continuous schedule is used at the 250 and 200 milisecond delay levels. For the 150–50 milisecond delay levels, the child receives a reinforcer at the end of each phrase. Tangible reinforcers are given during the treatment session. If they are tokens or chips they are redeemable for back-up reinforcers dependent upon each particular child. The chips, usually accumulated by the children very rapidly, are recorded as points on a data sheet using a ten to one schedule. For example, ten chips equal to one point. Some children spend their points in a speech store, where toys, games and prizes are displayed on five cabinet shelves. Items of least value are on the first shelf and items of most value are on the fifth shelf. Each child or each group of children works with a specific exchange schedule. For example, the items on the lowest shelf may cost ten points (100 chips or correct responses). By including the parent and the child in designing the back-up reinforcement schedule, the likelihood of the items actually serving as reinforcers is increased. Children and parents often create novel and unusual back-up items that function as effective reinforcers; the therapist would not think of these items because of her limited contact with the child. For example, one child suggested that he wanted to earn points so that his mother would let him keep the straw wrapper from the straw he received in the hospital cafeteria after each therapy session. Other children have requested going to the local museum of science and industry, having a friend spend the night, visiting their grandparents, seeing a movie, eating a pizza, and so forth.

Children learn to produce elements of normal speech under conditions of delayed auditory feedback.

Either system (the clinic speech store or the parent–child designed home system) or a combination of both may be used, depending on the child's needs. An item is a reinforcer only if the child increases his production of the target behavior as a result of its contingent availability. It has been said that therapy is the search for the right reinforcer. By giving the child a variety of options in the clinic and by including the parent and the child in the design of the home reinforcement system, the opportunity for reinforcers to be available is increased.

The Parent Program

During Phase I of the Child Stuttering Program, the parents meet for group therapy sessions. A client-centered therapy format is used to encourage parents to express feelings and beliefs about the child's problem and the treatment program. Topics such as the family schedule, the child's communicative opportunities, school behavior, reactions of siblings and significant others, procedures used to discipline the child, and strategies parents have used in the past to correct the child's speech are probed. Although the therapist is a

Date	Condition	Accum Time	Points Earned / Points Accum		Points Spent	Points Saved

Figure   4.2   *Child Stuttering Program: Phase I—Record of Progress*

member of the group and is available to answer questions and provide information, she basically plays as much of a non-directive role as possible. Often the parent, as well as the child, is hopeful that the therapist will be able to take the problem away magically and would prefer to relinquish all responsibility and associated worry to the therapist. With the therapist remaining basically non-directive in the group sessions, the parents begin to realize their own importance in these problem-solving activities. They begin to help each other develop coping strategies, attitudes, and beliefs that will encourage the child's permanent and durable behavior change. This kind of empathetic support on the part of the parent becomes critical when he is trained to implement the therapy program at home.

The Phase I activities described so far for developing volitional control of speech are of a general programmatic nature. Individual stutterers react differently to the tasks set before them during Phase I. The following section lists some of these individual variations and reactions.

WHAT IF MY STUTTERER . . .

Stutters when he starts to talk on the DAF machine?

In some instances the stutterer may not know how to start. Sometimes by giving the stutterer an example of slow, stretched out, and prolonged speech, he starts the process easily. If he still has trouble you proceed through the following steps:

1. Reading prose. (If he still stutters go to Step 2.)
2. Reading single, one syllable words. (If he still stutters go to Step 3.)
3. Prolonging isolated voiced phonemes.

If he can handle Step 3, have him combine prolonged phonemes into nonsense syllables and then proceed again through Steps 2 and 1 to open conversation.

Can't think of anything to talk about?

Ask him what he thinks would be the easiest thing for him to talk about. If he gives you a topic (e.g., sports, weather, politics, etc.) ask him what might be a little more difficult, and then even more difficult in terms of his expectancy to stutter, personal significance, or along any dimension of difficulty he may use. Ask him for such topics until you have six different ones.

If he can't provide topics in this fashion for himself, then you might suggest some, such as family, stuttering, himself, goals and aspirations, school, job, religion and beliefs, friends, and social activities.

Devise a grid that shows him that he will be asked to talk about each topic, under conditions of DAF and the appropriate contingencies for a minimum of five minutes, totaling 30 minutes, at each DAF interval. (Table 4.1)

As he completes five minutes of stutter-free speech on a topic at each interval, a check mark is placed in that cell. This should be explained to him and he should see it happening. With the completion of 30 minutes of talking on various topics at the slowest DAF interval, the DAF interval is changed from 250, to 200, etc., through 50. The stutterer should always have the freedom to talk on a topic as long as he wishes, or to choose any topic not on the list. This grid of topics is a mechanism to help get the stutterer started. Usually, he will quickly abandon this system for a less formal, less structured approach for helping him.

Table   4.1

Topic	250	200	150	100	50
1. Family	✓	✓✓			
2. Self	✓	✓			
3. Stuttering and speech	✓	✓✓			
4. The meaning of stutter-free speech	✓	✓	✓✓✓✓ ✓✓		
5. Friends and social activities	✓				
6. School	✓				

Seems to be disregarding the delayed signal and is talking too fast?

Ask him to talk slowly enough to eliminate the echo that he is hearing.

Prolongs each word appropriately but pauses in a staccato fashion between words?

Have the stutterer read a list of single words. Then ask him to read two-word units in which he *joins* the two words as though they were one word, for example:

1. jumble
   it
   jumbleit
2. give
   me
   giveme
3. tomorrow
   is
   tomorrowis

When the stutterer can do this, move on to three-word units, for example:

1. give me the
   givemethe
2. How are you
   Howareyou

After the stutterer can do this, go on to reading phrases in this same slowed down and combined fashion, involving continuous phonation. From this step, go back to free conversation.

Develops a type of metronomic beat in his speech so that there is a recurring monotonous rhythm?

Merely ask the stutterer to talk with his usual natural melody, inflection, and stress to prolong and stretch only the stressed words without stretching the small unstressed words.

Sometimes you can give the stutterer some examples, such as:

1. How *aŕe* you
2. How are *yoú*
3. Come and *seé* me
4. Come and see *mé*
5. *Coŕne* and *seé* me

This type of effect is observed more often at the slower DAF levels and usually disappears without any special attention at the faster levels. If it persists into DAF levels of 100 and 50 msec., you might well attend to the matter.

Has good continuous phonation between words, but blocks at the beginning of his utterance so that no sound is uttered?

When this happens it's usually on initial plosive sounds. Have the stutterer start his phonation or voicing before he starts to emit the main part of the phoneme. In other words, break the phoneme up into its micro elements. In a sense, it means extending phnonation backwards, before the phoneme is produced, for example:

1. mmmboy   (*m* for *p* and *b*)
2. mmmpie
3. nndo   (*n* for *t* and *d*)
4. nntip
5. nggoing   (*ng* for *g* and *k*)
6. ngcouple

For all other sounds, the stutterer needs to practice prolonging and stretching the initial sound and moving forward to the next sound.

Thinks that it's the DAF machine and not he himself that is slowing down his speech?

As the stutterer completes 30 minutes of stutter-free, slowed down, and continuously phonated speech at each DAF interval, turn off the DAF machine and have the stutterer replicate the same pattern of talking as if the DAF machine was in operation.

Table 4.2 Summary of Steps in Phase I Basic Therapy Paradigm

Step	Task for Client Speaking Stutter-Free	Condition	Time	Target Behavior	Contingency for Off Target Response	Reinforcement for Target Behavior
1	30 wpm, CP	250 msec. delay on DAF	30 min.	Rate, CP	5 extra training min.	Verbal praise
2	30 wpm, CP	w/o DAF signal	1 min.	Rate, CP	Reinstruct correct behavior and repeat	Verbal praise
3	45 wpm, CP suprasegmentals	200 msec. delay	30 min.	Rate, CP Prosody Inflect	5 extra training min.	Verbal praise
4	45 wpm, CP suprasegmentals	w/o DAF signal	1 min.	Rate, CP Prosody Inflect	Reinstruct correct behavior and repeat	Verbal praise
5	60 wpm, CP suprasegmentals	150 msec. delay	30 min.	Rate, CP Prosody Inflect	Reinstruct correct behavior and repeat	Verbal praise
6	60 wpm, CP suprasegmentals	w/o DAF signal	1 min.	Rate, CP Prosody Inflect	Reinstruct correct behavior and repeat	Verbal praise
7	75 wpm, CP suprasegmentals	100 msec. delay	30 min.	Rate, CP Prosody Inflect	Reinstruct correct behavior and repeat	Verbal praise
8	75 wpm, CP suprasegmentals	w/o DAF signal	1 min.	Rate, CP Prosody Inflect	Reinstruct correct behavior and repeat	Verbal praise

9	90 wpm, CP suprasegmentals	50 msec. delay	30 min.	Rate, CP Prosody Inflect	Reinstruct correct behavior and repeat	Verbal praise
10	90 wpm, CP suprasegmentals	w/o DAF signal	1 min.	Rate, CP Prosody Inflect	Reinstruct correct behavior and repeat	Verbal praise
11	30 wpm-90 wpm CP, suprasegmentals	w/250-50 msec. delay	2-3 min.	Rate, CP Prosody Inflect	Reinstruct correct behavior and repeat	Verbal praise
12	30 wpm-90 wpm CP, suprasegmentals	w/o DAF signal	2-3 min.	Rate, CP Prosody Inflect	Reinstruct correct behavior and repeat	Verbal praise

Materials Needed:

1. Clock/Stopwatch
2. DAF machine or equivalent
3. Data sheet

WPM   Words per minute
CP   Continuous phonation
DAF   Delayed auditory feedback

Table 4.3 Summary of Steps in Phase I Child Therapy Paradigm

Step	Task for Client Speaking Stutter-Free	Condition	Time	Target Behavior	Contingency for Off-Target Responses	Reinforcement for Target Behavior
1	30 wpm Rate CP	250 msec. delay on DAF	15 min. (5 min. units)	Rate, CP	Loss of talking turn	1 chip 2-word unit
2	45 wpm Rate CP	200 msec. delay	15 min. (5 min. units)	Rate, CP	Loss of talking turn	1 chip 2-word unit
3	60 wpm Rate CP, suprasegmental	150 msec. delay	15 min. (5 min. units)	Rate, CP Pros., Inflect	Loss of talking turn	1 chip/ phrase
4	75 wpm Rate CP, suprasegmental	100 msec. delay	15 min. (5 min. units)	Rate, CP Pros., Inflect	Loss of talking turn	1 chip/ phrase
5	90 wpm Rate CP, Suprasegmental	50 msec. delay	15 min. (5 min. units)	Rate, CP Pros., Inflect	Loss of talking turn	1 chip/ phrase

Materials Needed:

1. Language stimulation materials (sequence pictures, games)
2. Timer
3. DAF machine or equivalent   Date Sheet #_____

Chapter 5

Phase II Self Reinforcement

Introduction

Although each phase of the therapy contributes its own unique features to the overall program, and each phase depends on the preceding phase and integrates with the succeeding phase, *Phase II: Self Reinforcement* has a significance that goes beyond the phases of therapy. Eventually, the client finds herself on her own, depending on herself and making crucial judgments about what she should do. She has to reason, problem solve, and become responsible for herself. These responsibilities are far reaching. Some may focus quite specifically on the stuttering problem, but others may deal with general goals, expectations, decisions, and actions that may encompass social interactions, education, and occupation. Becoming responsible for one's self in a general way may relate to a general pattern of self responsibility that each of us over the years may have developed. On the other hand, our tendencies toward self responsibility may vary with the kinds of situations we find ourselves in and how comfortable we are with ourselves under certain circumstances.

It appears that some people have a strong tendency to manage their affairs with very little outside support, structure, or feedback, while others need a great deal of external control, support, and feedback. One of the features of this therapy for stuttering is that it provides specific and formal training in the processes of self reinforcement. This is part of a regime of self regulation that the stutterer faces in her next phase of therapy and may face after therapy is formally terminated.

The structure of this phase of the therapy is based partially on the theory of Kanfer and Karoly (1972). It states that self regulation has three elements: monitoring, evaluation, and reinforcement.

The goals of Phase II are to train the client to independently:

1. self-instruct behavioral responses
2. self-monitor her behavior
3. self-evaluate her behavior
4. self-consequate her behavior

During this training phase, the responsibility for each of the components of the self regulation process is transferred from clinician to client control.

Initially, the clinician presents an overt signal, such as a hand raised to instruct the subject to produce a slow rate with continuous phonation. A hand lowered indicates a faster rate with continuous phonation. This instruction functions as an S^D for the behavior of deliberate monitored speech. The client then produces the instructed speech behavior and it is tape recorded. After listening to the tape recorded speech behavior, the clinician and client evaluate her produc-

The client learns self-regulatory behaviors.

tion of instructed rate and continuous phonation. After the client successfully produces and evaluates her target behavior, she also assumes responsibility for self instruction. The self instruction signal is
reduced to a more covert motoric movement (such as a socially acceptable gesture or raised finger) so it becomes totally unnoticeable to a
listener. The very slow rate of speech is faded out systematically,
leaving only a socially acceptable rate of talking. The client is now
trained to self-instruct, to monitor, and to self-evaluate her monitored
speech behavior. She is now ready to self-consequate her speech behavior. We have arbitrarily selected unmonitored speech as a reinforcer. Premack (1959) states that a high frequency behavior can function as a reinforcer if it is made contingent on the emission of a low
frequency target behavior. Because unmonitored speech is highly desired by our clients and is a high frequency behavior for all speakers,
we have selected this behavior to serve as a reinforcer for monitored
speech. Also, because it is under the control of the stutterer, unmonitored speech is appropriate as a self-reinforcer rather than as an externally provided reinforcer. Therefore, the client is now able to engage in all four self regulatory behaviors as follows:

1. Self Instruction   Motoric signal to emit monitored or unmonitored speech

2. Self Monitoring   Client deliberately emits socially acceptable
rate and continuous phonation

3. Self Evaluation   Client self-evaluates correctness of her
response

4. Self Consequation   Client rewards herself with unmonitored
speech

The goals are:

1. To establish independent volitional control of the speech response.
2. To establish a monitored, normal-sounding speech response.
3. To train elements of self reinforcement.

The Treatment Paradigm

Once the client has completed Phase I training, she has developed the ability to produce stutter-free speech at a slightly slowed-down rate under clinician controlled contingencies. During Phase II, a systematic transfer of the reinforcement system takes place from clinician to client management. The first session of phase two begins with a brief review of the DAF levels. At each level, the client begins to produce conversational speech with the loudness of the feedback at the regular volume. As the client continues to speak, the loudness is decreased and the client attempts to maintain consistent rate and continuous phonation. The loudness is increased and decreased at the various DAF levels until the client begins to feel comfortable maintaining the target behaviors with or without the DAF contingencies. The client is then instructed to vary the loudness and delay levels herself while maintaining volitional control of the desired behavior. The client is then asked to produce a painfully slow rate of speech without the DAF machine. She is instructed to produce the rate she used at the 250 msec. delay level. The clinician and client evaluate a tape recording of her speech response to determine the accuracy of volitional control of rate and continuous phonation. The client is then asked to produce a rate that is faster than the previous one but still slightly slower than she would like to speak. Again the client and the clinician evaluate the accuracy of the response. The clinician then determines signals that instruct the client to produce either the exaggerated slow rate or the slightly slower rate. The client responds, and both the client and clinician evaluate the accuracy of the response. As the client becomes skilled in correct production of her behaviors, the clinician instructs the client to self-instruct her own motor speech behavior. At this point the client begins to assume independent responsibility for self evaluation of the response. Finally, use of the tape recorder is also discontinued and the client is then able to self-instruct, self-monitor, and self-evaluate her motor speech behavior.

The last step in Phase II training is to change the source and form of reinforcement. The client is trained to insert very brief units of unmonitored speech (four or five words) as a reinforcer for appropriate signalling, continuous phonation, and slightly slower rate of speaking. At first, these insertions of unmonitored speech are signalled by the clinician for about 20% of the stutterer's speech output. Eventually, the signalling for such insertions of unmonitored speech is managed by the client. It is interesting that gradually these in-

stances of unmonitored speech begin to resemble the rate and phonation characteristics of the client's monitored portions of talking. This
occurs because of generalization of the elements of the two ways of
talking (monitored and unmonitored). However, this is usually not observed until the later stages of Phase III during Environmental Transfer.

The Speech Stimuli

Often conversational speech is too complex a response for the initial
Phase II training. Therefore, simple sentences or reading material may
be used to control level of difficulty. It may be necessary to practice
inflection and phrasing drills to insure appropriate suprasegmental
behavior. As the client becomes skilled in each aspect of the self reinforcement paradigm, the clinician may increase the complexity of the
speech activity until conversational speech is achieved. This conversational practice is usually continued for one entire session of an
hour's length. It is extended in its operation into Phase III, Transfer,
but it is not usually the focus of attention at that point.

Child Program

Many times the child comes to the clinic expecting the therapist to
cure her stuttering. Unfortunately, the therapist will not be able to
satisfy her desire. He will be able to teach the child to produce new
speech behaviors that are incompatible with stuttering, but ultimately
the child alone must choose to produce these behaviors on a permanent basis. Thus, we want to encourage as much self responsibility
for the child as early as possible. Even in Phase I, activities such as
recording time earned on DAF, clocking the time on a stopwatch, and
dispensing reinforcement become the responsibilities of the children.

Children learn self-regulatory behaviors.

While one child is engaged in learning volitional control of speech, another child is given time-keeper responsibility, another records on the daily data profile, and another gives the chips. In this way, the children gain an empirical understanding of each variable that is important in this part of the program. They begin to realize that therapy is not the sole responsibility of the therapist.

In this phase of the program the child learns to implement the four elements of the self reinforcement paradigm: self instruction, self monitoring, self evaluation, and self consequation of her own speech behavior.

Self Instruction and Monitoring

Initially, we want the child to be able to select specific speech responses and produce them correctly. Therefore, in Step 1 of this phase, selected speech responses made by the child are carefully measured. The child produces a minute of spontaneous speech under conditions of 250, 150, 50 msec. delay, while the therapist counts the number of words emitted during the one-minute period on a digital counter. These baseline measurements signify very slow, medium slow, and slightly slow rates. The therapist explains to the child the number of words per minute she produced at each rate.

In Step 2, the therapist repeats Step 1 for the first 30 seconds of the 1-minute sample. During the second 30 seconds, the child attempts to maintain her rate and continuous phonation as the therapist continues to measure the child's successful completion of the task by counting the number of words per minute. The therapist provides feedback for the child in several ways. First he gives her the target number words per minute obtained from her base rate as a goal. Secondly, he tells her the number of words per minute she produces on each 1-minute trial. In this way the child begins to develop a sense of careful volitional control of her own speech rate. For any 1-minute trial, she knows if she produces more or less words per minute than her base rate target behavior, she is then easily able to modify her behavior accordingly. Although the child is concentrating on learning her rate, she must also continue to produce the other elements of stutter-free speech: continuous phonation and intact suprasegmental structure. If these elements of her new speech response are produced correctly, she receives one chip per phrase. The child must achieve correct 1-minute trials for each rate before she can advance to the next step. Thus, the child begins to understand a variety of different specific rates and learns to self-monitor target elements of her new speech response.

In Step 3, the therapist fades the duration of the DAF stimulus signal from the initial 30 second period until it is completely faded. The child may choose her desired rate for her 1-minute trial. She receives feedback on her ability to produce correct rate, phonation, and suprasegmental features by viewing the counter for the WPM and by receiving a positive reinforcer for each correct phrase. By the end of Step 3, the child is able to independently self-instruct the three rates. While she produces her response, she has learned to independently self-monitor her rate, phonation, and suprasegmentals correctly. For the first three steps the therapist engages the children in a variety of structured language activities, such as describing sequence or activity stimulus cards. These speech tasks are selected so that they can be controlled by the therapist. The child needs to be provided a stimulus that will evoke 1 minute of speech only. Therefore, the therapist would not choose to involve the children in making plays or puppet shows at this time. The children need to take turns for each 1-minute speech trial, so the therapist needs to exert ample control over the speaking situation.

At this point, we are ready to help the child shape her target responses so they more closely approximate normal speech. During Step 4, the child is asked to produce two rates: the slow rate is a 50 wpm rate and the fast rate is a 90 wpm rate. The therapist will initially signal which rate is desired from the child. However, the child quickly assumes responsibility for self instruction. The child engages in a conversational speech activity in which she self-instructs slow or fast speech by producing an overt signal, such as raising her hand and producing the correct behavior. The therapist evaluates all elements of her stutter-free speech response by giving her one chip per phrase. The child is instructed to alternate between the two rates, with about seven or eight words per rate. During Step 4, the therapist moves the children away from the highly structured activities they engaged in earlier, to more natural communication interactions such as plays and puppet shows. The children are still able to earn one chip per phrase. Typically, the therapist is seated, dispenses chips for each child, and records the number of correct responses on a data sheet. The therapist has a stack of 10 chips for each child on a table beside him. When a child earns a chip, he moves it from its original stack to create a new stack. Placing the chip on the table after the child's response makes a noise, indicating to her that she received a chip. After the child earns the stack of 10 chips: she receives a point on her data sheet.

Self Evaluation and Consequation

During the first four steps the children have learned to independently self-instruct and self-monitor the elements of their new motor speech behavior. The therapist has continued to provide feedback regarding correct production of the response and dispensed appropriate reinforcement. During Step 5, the child learns to assume responsibility for independently evaluating and consequating her own behavior. The children are again engaged in a structured language activity. The child signals a specific rate, and produces her speech behavior for a 30 second period that is tape recorded. She then listens to her own speech and decides whether or not she produced her speech correctly.

Name _____

	1	2	3	4	5	6	7	8	9	10	11	12	13	14	15	16	17	18	19	20	Total Correct
Rate																					
CP																					
Inflection																					
Rate																					
CP																					
Inflection																					
Rate																					
CP																					
Inflection																					
Rate																					
CP																					
Inflection																					
Rate																					
CP																					
Inflection																					
Rate																					
CP																					
Inflection																					
Rate																					
CP																					
Inflection																					
Rate																					
CP																					
Inflection																					

Figure 5.1 *Scoring Form for Phase II*

She records her evaluation on the data recording form shown in Figure 5.1. She must decide if she produced the correct rate and if her continuous phonation and inflection were good. If she produced all three elements correctly, she takes a chip for herself. The child must have four consecutive correct trials before advancing.

Conclusion

The goals of Phase II are to learn to self-instruct, self-monitor, self-evaluate, and self-consequate one's own behavior. It means that the client learns to become responsible for herself and for managing major aspects of her therapy. We have tried to differentiate high self reinforcers from low self reinforcers and to account for their differing kinds of responsiveness to this phase of their therapy. Some clients will have to be nurtured through this phase while others eagerly take hold of their own destinies.

When this phase of therapy was first conceived and applied it was highly regulated and structured into very small gradual steps, or trials. The clinician instructed a certain number of trials and then gradually turned this behavior over to the client. For example, six monitoring trials of instruction were provided by the clinician and none by the client; then five instructional trials by the clinician and one by the client; then four by the clinician and two by the client, until eventually all monitoring trials were instructed by the client. This pattern of scheduling the trials was repeated for evaluating and for consequating until the client had the full responsibility for each step in the self reinforcement paradigm. However, we found later that this rather rigorous approach was not generally necessary and was only used when a client was having trouble with a particular element of the paradigm.

The following section lists some of the things that we have encountered as the clients progressed through this phase of the therapy. They are common enough to alert the reader to their possible occurrence and to describe what we have done about them.

WHAT IF MY STUTTERER . . .

Stutters during unmonitored speech?

We usually ask the client to reduce the amount of unmonitored speech she is using as a reinforcer. Sometimes we go back to tighten up the monitoring and slow down the rate or examine the quality of her continuous phonation. We also have practiced the monitoring by alternating the 250—50 msec. delay and associated rate of speech, both on and off the DAF machine.

Signals the behavior but does not emit that behavior?

We usually ask the client to shorten the target behavior and to decrease the intervals between signalling, thereby increasing the frequency of signalling behavior. The clinician quickly evaluates the behavior, very early in the utterance.

Gradually permits his slow rate of speech to become too fast?

We put the client back on the DAF machine at various levels and tape record her speech for home practice. At she listens and approximates what she hears on the tape recorder. She actually counts the number of words and attenuates her speech to the appropriate rate for her monitoring.

Is distracted by the content of what she is talking about?

We have reverted to selective topics progressing from lesser to greater interest or linguistic complexity. Occasionally we have resorted to oral reading.

Emits too long a response before she evaluates it?

We usually ask the client to shorten the target behavior and to decrease the intervals between signalling, thereby increasing the frequency of signalling. The clinician quickly evaluates the behavior, very early in the utterance.

Stutters during monitored speech?

We ask the stutterer to slow her rate and to re-examine her continuous phonation. We sometimes go back on the DAF machine and alternate between talking at 250 msec. and 50 msec. We then practice that rate off of the DAF machine.

Doesn't change promptly from one behavior to another?

This is similar to the second point. Under these circumstances the clinician takes over the signalling and evaluating, permitting the client to concentrate only on emitting the appropriate behaviors.

Perseverates on very slow monitored speech and is afraid to monitor at a faster rate?

Ask the stutterer to talk as fast as she can to demonstrate the broad speed limits for talking in phrases without stuttering.

Wants to signal covertly, too soon?

Explain the initial need to make the signal explicit and that it is too tempting to discard signalling as a part of the paradigm. Without the signal, monitoring becomes accidental, random, or used only when stuttering is anticipated.

Permits her speech to get too choppy?

Have the client engage in phrasing exercises, prolonging single words, then two-word units, three-word units, and whole phrases until her speech is smooth. The whole phrase should be viewed as a single word.

Says that she plans her entire statement before she says it because she can't talk and think about her speech at the same time?

We have reverted to selective topics progressing from lesser to greater interest or linguistic complexity. Occasionally we have resorted to oral reading.

Evalutes incorrectly?

The clinician assumes the evaluation behavior and calibrates the client to the clinician's criteria.

Evaluates speech as being too slow and therefore unacceptable?

This is related to the previous point. However, in this instance we use much modelling with a tape recorder to reach a decision of an acceptable rate.

Resurrects old speech behaviors such as circumlocutions?

Often this is done almost unconsciously during unmonitored speech. The client should be highly conscious of this behavior. We have used negative practice, followed by instructions to actually inhibit the behavior.

Anticipates and tracks failure (stuttering) in spite of successful monitoring?

We have used mild verbal disapproval, rejecting comments about stuttering, and verbal approval, accepting comments about monitoring the target behaviors.

Begins to talk like a robot?

We instruct the stutterer to not prolong unstressed words in the phrase or let go of the small connecting words. We have also used inflection and stress exercises.

Table 5.1 Summary of Steps in Phase II Basic Therapy Paradigm

Step	Training Task	Condition	Time	Target Behavior	Contingency for Off-Target Response	Reinforcement
1	Volitional control of motor speech response	Clinician signals, monitors, evaluates & consequates	5 min.	30-60-90 wpm CP Supra segmentals	Return to DAF	Verbal praise
2	Self instruction	Client signals, and monitors Clinician evaluates & consequates	5 min.	30-60-90 wpm CP Supra segmentals	Return to DAF	Verbal praise
3	Self monitoring and evaluation	Client signals, monitors and evaluates (tape recorder) Clinician consequates	5 min.	30-60-90 wpm CP Supra segmentals	Return to DAF	Verbal praise
4	Self consequation	Clinician signals self rf paradigm	5 min.	90 wpm-UnM	Return to slower rates	UnM
5.	Self consequation	Client controls self rf paradigm		90 wpm-UnM	Return to slower rates	UnM

wpm   words per minute
CP   continuous phonation
rf   reinforcement
UnM   unmonitored speech

Table 5.2 Summary of Steps in Phase II Child Therapy Paradigm

Step	Task	Condition	Time	Trial Behavior	Contingency for Off-Target Response	Reinforcement
1	Base Rate WPM	DAF 250 150 50	1 min. trial	Correct rate and CP		
2	Self instruction, monitoring	DAF 250 150 50	1 min. trial 30 sec. with DAF 30 sec. without DAF	Correct rate and CP	Increase period of DAF	1 chip per phase
3	Self instruction, monitoring	DAF 250 150 50	1 min. trial fade DAF	Correct rate and CP	Return to Step 2 above	1 chip per phase
4	Self instruction, monitoring	Alternating slow/fast rates independently	Conversational interaction	Correct rate and CP	Return to Step 3 above	1 chip per phase
5	Self evaluation, consequation	slow/fast rates	30 sec. trials	Correct rate and CP	Return to Step 4 above	1 chip per phase

Chapter 6

Phase III   Transfer

Introduction

Once the client is able to self-instruct, self-monitor, self-evaluate, and self-consequate his newly learned stutter-free speech behaviors, he is ready to address transfer of training. For most clients the first two phases of therapy follow a relatively consistent pattern in terms of time for treatment criterion and manner of response acquisition. However, the transfer of training period tends to vary a great deal from client to client. The purpose of this phase is to facilitate the client's ability to develop strategies for incorporating monitored stutter-free speech into his total life systems. For some individuals this type of transfer requires changes in many other complex aspects of his personality style, self-concept, and coping mechanisms.

The Emotional Aspects of Transfer

As a stutterer, the client may have continually questioned the etiology and nature of his problem, as well as potential courses of treatment, to no avail. This frightening state of uncertainty about all aspects of his problem leads him to see himself as the helpless victim of a mysterious, undefined malady. Therefore, he often thinks his speech is controlled by his environment. From his point of view his vocal mechanism has operated outside his control, almost as if his speech musculature were controlled by forces separate from the rest of his body. Furthermore, his inability to communicate effectively may isolate the stutterer from society. Because he is unable to convey his message, or because he feels embarrassed and fears what might happen if he attempts to talk, the stutterer may avoid many speaking situations. As a result, we have seen many adult clients who have *never* had a date or a close friend. Many have never spoken to anyone at school, recited in class, engaged in any extra curricular activities, or have even said more than one or two sentences at a time to their parents and family. Although the stutterer may excel academically, he may experience marked difficulty in the job market. He may be unable to face a job interview and, because most jobs require a great deal of verbal interactions, will not qualify for the job if he is unable to communicate. Many stutterers have been markedly underemployed if employed at all. Thus, as the stutterer observes the non-stutterer living a much more complex and complete social and vocational life, he may feel a great deal of anger and self-pity over his unfair plight.

When the stutterer begins to change his speech, these other aspects of his life may be subject to change concomitantly. Giving up stuttering may mean giving up his primary coping or defense mechanism for self protection. Fear of failure may predominate when he considers attempting the social and vocational interactions he has consistently avoided in the past. He has learned to relate to people from a posture of his own weakness, rather than from a posture of his strengths. As a result, he has been reinforced by listeners for playing

a role of the weak victim. In this role, he is not threatened nor interrupted in his talking; not only has he lowered his own expectations,
but those with whom he interacts have also lowered his expectations.
This posture is far different than a posture of strength (normal
speech), where expectations are perhaps higher and qualitatively
different, where relations develop that involve the unmasked person un-
derneath, the real person that is in each of us. It is a posture of
strength where stuttering is not a factor in his success or failure as a
human being. A posture of weakness can be deeply imbedded in the
stutterer's self concept, in his overt behaviors, and in his dynamic
coping strategies. The rewards of being nurtured by others, of having
an excuse for failure, and of feeling helpless and victimized are part of
the investment in his problem that the stutterer must make some decisions about. Does he hang on to these rewards of weakness and try
to continue to function in this weak mode, or does he give these
things up for the rewards that may accrue with stutter-free speech?
These decisions are difficult and are usually re-examined throughout
therapy, as the stutterer experiences the consequences of stuttered
and stutter-free speech. Deciding to change his manner of talking becomes a much bigger choice than merely electing a new motor-speech
response. For many clients it means changing every aspect of their
lives.

The Dualistic Aspects of Transfer

In the transfer phase of therapy the client begins to use his new monitored stutter-free speech socially, on a gradual and systematic basis.
At first he emits his new monitored speech for perhaps three 5-minute
periods each day. Although the amount of stutter-free talking time,
both monitored and unmonitored, increases each day, during much of
the day he is using his old way of talking, probably stuttering as he always did. Thus, he experiences a very strange dualistic existence.

On the one hand, he experiences relaxed monitored stutter-free
speech with his clinician in therapy and then short periods of deliberate monitored stutter-free speech in his nonclinical environment. On the other hand, during the rest of the time, he is his old self:
a stuttering, avoiding, helpless, lonely, isolated, and angry individual.
He is coping as he has always coped, using those mechanisms he has
developed for his survival. As we recognize that his therapeutic experience is superimposed on his everyday life, we acknowledge that he
is not immune to the problems, stresses, and normal development of
non-stutterers. A child may reasonably be clinging to the safety and
protection of his parents. An adolescent may be exploring the world
outside his family as he seeks separate identity and independence
while he responds to the mores of his peers. The adult may have very
strongly established patterns of coping. It is within the context of the
stutterer's continued participation in society, in his family, in school,
and on the job that his speech therapy operates. He may have doubts

about the outcome, be suspicious of too quick a change, and be fearful of new and more demanding expectations of himself as a former stutterer. He may then resist sacrificing the years of emotional investment and coping that involved his problem. Going from the known, where he understands the ground rules for his problem, to the unknown can be frightening. In therapy, the stutterer may have a special set of problems relating to that therapy. For him, relapse may be lurking around the corner. Perhaps he is afraid to hope and work toward a goal that has eluded him for years. These feelings and fears and hopes are a part of his therapy and accompany the behavioral regime he experiences with his clinician. This period of transition from who and what he is (or identifies himself as) to who he finally becomes is fraught with conflict, regrets, guilts, and a certain amount of nostalgia. There is a mixture of fear and hope about the future.

For many clients, the environmental transfer phase of the treatment program is a particular period where new personality dynamics appear to emerge. As the client accumulates stutter-free speech experiences, he also attempts speaking in situations he may have feared or avoided in the past. These experiences may involve social or vocational interactions unique to the client's history. Thus, as the client continues to increase his transfer activities, components of self concept and self perception begin to change in concert with his new experiences. The client does not arrange his transfer activities in a hierarchy of easy to severe situations. Instead, he attempts to remain at a comfortable level at all times while continuing to slowly but steadily shape the response until he is able to successfully monitor his new speech behavior in all communicative interactions. During the transfer period, we have found that strict compliance to a carefully planned monitoring schedule with consistent self-evaluation and reinforcement is very important. The client selects a transfer schedule that reflects a minimal and comfortable commitment to incorporating his new behaviors into his environment. Thus, during initial activity, the client may plan to monitor stutter-free speech for as little as three social interactions during the day, totaling perhaps 5 to 10 minutes of talking time. By design, the client does not attempt to monitor his speech for all other speech acts, although he is free to do so if he wishes. During therapy and specific transfer activities he behaves as a stutter-free speaker, with monitored, fluent speech; the rest of the day he may well behave as a stutterer. The client is now able to make choices about his speech. When he adheres to his transfer schedule, he chooses to speak without stuttering and begins to sense a feeling of control over his speech that he never before experienced. Clients typically report that this feeling of control is indeed powerful, so much so that they begin to believe that they are able to control other aspects of their lives that previously were controlled by the fact that they stuttered. Initially, during transfer, for a limited time, the client interacts without stuttering and experiences a feeling of control over his behavior; during the rest of the day he produces his previous behavior. As a result, many clients have reported feeling like two people inside one body: the new person, capable of stutter-free speech, eager to attempt new social and vocational interactions, and willing to control his own destiny; and the old person, stuttering, avoiding interactions, feeling a helpless victim of his stuttering, and resisting therapy or resisting moving forward in therapy. One client even stated that for a while he felt as though the two personalities were waging war over whether or not he should come to therapy. It appears that the new person desires completion of the treatment program vehemently, while the old person fears intensely the changes in behavior he feels would be necessary if he no longer stuttered. These changes in personality dynamics appear to occur only after monitored stutter-free speech has been established and the transfer phase is initiated. Therefore, the development of an appropriate therapeutic relationship is critical so that the clinician and the client can explore and problem solve these incongruities together.

When we accept the responsibility for dealing with a stutterer's problems, we are accepting a responsibility for more than merely applying some effective conditioning operations or behavioral modification tactics. We are concerned with more than those changes in speech occurring in our office. We are also responsible for helping the stutterer to assimilate these changes and to integrate them into his total intrapsychic and interpersonal condition. What has loosely been referred to as *carryover* involves the total person, not merely his speech. It involves an environmental generalization of new speaking skills; it also involves the stutterer's reactions to these experiences.

Evoking a single instance of stutter-free speech is a relatively uncomplicated and easy operation for both the clinician and the stutterer. *Instating* stutter-free speech in a controlled environment may depend more on operant conditioning tactics than any other aspect of therapy. However, *environmental transfer* may depend mostly on the therapeutic relationship that has evolved. It is in this phase of therapy that client-change is most validly facilitated and evaluated.

The Treatment Paradigm

The Contract

The goal of Phase III of the treatment program is to transfer the newly trained speech behaviors environmentally. Because this newly trained behavior is yet somewhat fragile and the possibility of an interruption in the client's ability to concentrate on producing his new complex of behaviors may arise from a number of environmental variables, a highly systematic, preplanned environmental transfer structure has been developed. This transfer plan is in the form of a contract. With the contract, the client predetermines the exact time, place, listener, and his own behavior plan for using his new speech behavior environmentally. For example, the client may decide to speak to a specifically designated co-worker for 2 to 3 minutes during their 10:00 A.M. coffee break in the cafeteria. In addition, the client designs his own behavior plan. In other words, he writes out his plan for self instructing his desired motor response. Depending on the terminology and concepts used in the self-reinforcement phase of therapy, his plan may be as follows:

1. Signal: monitored speech for initial 80% of each speech act.
2. Signal: unmonitored speech for final 20% of each speech act for a 2 to 3 minute conversation.

By defining as many variables as he can in formulating the contract, the client is essentially controlling his environment as much as possible. As a result, he is able to focus his concentration on programming his new motor speech responses as self-instructed by his behavior plan. The client's focus or concentration on programming the new behaviors replaces his automatic motor programming of old speech responses. By using the contract the client increases the probability of his instructing and emitting the desired behavior, stutter-free speech (controlled rate, continuous phonation, and forward moving speech). This contract represents the client's minimal commitment to the transfer of his stutter-free speech to the environment. It is based on the client's comfort level about those activities. The client can go beyond the elements of his contract if he so chooses. However, frequency and duration of monitored speech, speaking situation, and audience are varied until the client's entire talking day is monitored stutter-free speech, and a wide variety of conversational interactions have been successfully completed. Individuals vary in how they implement this phase and in how rapidly they expand their contract. Typically, the contract is drawn up each morning and the client reviews the day's activities each night, usually by tape recording his review of the day. This contract activity is reviewed with the clinician during the following therapy session.

Before the client begins to attempt environmental contracts, several variables need to be considered. For the most part, clients are very eager to try this new way of talking outside the clinic. The changes in motor speech behavior have usually occurred very quickly and within about two weeks the client is speaking without stuttering, as does a normal speaker. The client may find it very difficult to accept so quick a change in the problem that he and probably many professionals have been trying to remedy for years. Because of the client's reinforcement history of unsuccessful speech attempts and his fear of change, it seems as though a part of him is waiting for failure or relapse. The other part realizes intellectually that he really understands the change in his speech and that the behavioral program he is involved in makes a lot of sense. This part of him is anxious for success.

It is important at this stage in the program for the clinician to satisfy two goals:

1. Permit the client to develop his own problem-solving strategy.
2. Facilitate the client's successful talking experiences.

To satisfy these goals the clinician must move in and out of several roles: counselor, teacher, and speech therapist. Sometimes the tactics of the clinician may conflict with the tactics the client wishes to explore. For example, if the client devises a contract activity that is within the general framework of the program but success seems doubtful, should the clinician as *counselor* permit the client to attempt the activity and risk failure, or should the clinician as *teacher* tell the client that his plan could be improved in a particular way? For the most part, we have found that the client will, with extra determination, engage in those activities he has designed and gut-level believes in instead of following the didactic instruction from the clinician. Because we would like to see the client make permanent, durable changes in his speech and self perception, we believe that the client needs the space and supportive environment for personal decision making and growth. Therefore, although within the session the clinician may non-directively help the client develop seemingly appropriate problem-solving strategies, the ultimate decisions are left to the client. In this way, the clinician reinforces the client by her belief in the client's ability to solve his own problems, to be responsible for himself, and to be in charge of his environment. It is within this client-centered behavioral context that the transfer process begins.

Because the client has seen a description of the contract activity on videotape during the initial session, the concept is not entirely foreign to him. In planning the transfer of training the client makes a series of decisions relative to taking stutter-free speech from the therapist and her office into everyday life. He begins to think about this transfer in terms of audience, location, situations, time of day, duration of speech act, verbal content, and excitement level. A hierarchy of speaking situations begins to emerge, not in the classical sense where situations are ranked from easy to difficult in regard to severity of stuttering, but wherein the client now attempts to isolate and order situations in which he will be able to concentrate on his self-reinforcement scheme. In doing so, situations in which he has never before stuttered may become most difficult. For example, if the client never stutters with his wife, he may experience difficulty maintaining concentration on his behavior plan because he does not foresee stuttering as a contingency. Because the goal of the program is total stutter-free speech, it is important that the client does not attempt to monitor his speech only when he thinks he will stutter. Most probably, what will result in this case would be a fluent stutterer, someone who emits special behaviors when he thinks he will stutter to avoid stuttering. Thus, a change in self concept in the environment would be difficult for the client to acquire because he would still be behaving as an abnormal speaker.

date & contract no.	person/audience	time	place	behavior plan	situation & difficulty (1-7)	name _____ page _____ / evaluation

Figure 6.1 Transfer Contract Record

name JANE DOE   page 1

date & contract no.	person/ audience	time	place	behavior plan	situation & difficulty (1-7)	evaluation
1. 8. 6	Sister	7°° 7°⁵	HOME	1. Signal 2. Slow Rate 3. Continuous Phonation 4. Unmonitored	1.	WENT PERFECTLY, SIGNALLED ALL THE TIME, WENT SLOW + USED CONTINUOUS PHONATION, + REMEMBERED TO UNMONITOR - GOOD CONTROL

name JANE DOE page 13

date & contract no.	person/ audience	time	place	behavior plan	situation & difficulty (1-7)	evaluation
37 8.31	Boss	9:00 9:30	OFFICE	1. SIGNAL 2. SLOW RATE 3. CONTINUOUS PHONATION 4. UNMONITOR	7	VERY DIFFICULT SITUATION, AND ALL BEHAVIORS WERE 100% NEXT WILL BEGIN MONITORING ALL DAY

Time	Monday	Tuesday	Wednesday	Thursday	Friday	Saturday	Sunday
8:00 – 8:30							
8:30– 9:00							
9:00– 9:30							
9:30–10:00							
10:00–10:30							
10:30–11:00							
11:00–11:30							
11:30–12:00							
12:00–12:30							
12:30– 1:00							
1:00– 1:30							
1:30– 2:00							
2:00– 2:30							
2:30– 3:00							

Figure   6.2   *Time Block Contract*

3:00- 3:30						
3:30- 4:00						
4:00- 4:30						
4:30- 5:00						
5:00- 5:30						
5:30- 6:00						
6:00- 6:30						
6:30- 7:00						
7:00- 7:30						
7:30- 8:00						
8:00- 8:30						
8:30- 9:00						
9:00- 9:30						
9:30-10:00						
10:00-10:30						
10:30-11:00						
11:00-11:30						
11:30-12:00						

	Monday	Tuesday	Wednesday	Thursday	Friday	Saturday	Sunday	
8:00- 8:30								
8:30- 9:00								
9:00- 9:30	Rate+ Phonation+	Rate +	Rate +	Rate +	Rate +			
9:30-10:00	Signal+	Phonation+	Phon. +	Phon.+	Phon.+			
10:00-10:30	Reward+	Signal+	Sig. +	Sig. +	Sig. +			
10:30-11:00		Reward+	Rew. +	Rew. +	Rew. +			
11:00-11:30								
11:30-12:00						Rate+		
12:00-12:30						Phon.+		
12:30- 1:00						Sig. +		
1:00- 1:30						Rew. +		
1:30- 2:00								
2:00- 2:30							Rate	+
2:30- 3:00							Phon.	+
3:00- 3:30							Sign.	+
3:30- 4:00							Rew.	+
4:00- 4:30								

4:30- 5:00							
5:00- 5:30	Rate+ ~~Phonation+~~	Rate+	Rate+	Rate+	Rate +		
5:30- 6:00	Signal +	Phonation+	Phon. −	Phon.+	Phon. +		
6:00- 6:30	Reward+	Signal+	Sig. +	Sig. +	Sig. +		
6:30- 7:00		Reward+	Rew. +	Rew. +	Rew. +		
7:00- 7:30							
7:30- 8:00							
8:00- 8:30							
8:30- 9:00							
9:00- 9:30							
9:30-10:00							
10:00-10:30							
10:30-11:00							
11:00-11:30							
11:30-12:00							
	Good day, all behavior 100%, will increase my time	GREAT- will increase	At 5³⁰ DID NOT BUMP WORDS PROPERLY STAY THE SAME FOR THURSDAY	GREAT, will increase	GREAT	WENT ALL DAY EXCEPT WHEN I FIRST GOT UP, 100%	ALL DAY 100%

Pre-Environmental Contract Activity

Generally, the client initially elects to attempt some practice contracts within the clinic. The client may vary specific location, audience, presence or absence of therapist, or situation within the clinical environment. For example, the client may make phone calls from the therapist's office, contract with other therapists or clinic staff members, or contract before small groups. During this pre-environmental contract activity, the therapist is close at hand, available to assist the client in contract design and evaluation. As the client progresses through these clinical contracts he begins to understand his current limitations in terms of duration of concentration time, verbal content, audience, and excitement level. Thus, the client experiences each aspect of the self-reinforcement scheme during this initial contract activity. He self-instructs his responses by designing and writing his contract plan; he self-monitors his behavior during the actual contract activity; he evaluates his performance in terms of successful completion of his behavior plan (not presence or absence of stuttering) and writes his evaluation on the contract recording form. He may evaluate his performance from his memory of the speaking situation or he may choose to tape record (when unobtrusive) the contract and evaluate the recording afterwards. The brief emission of unmonitored speech serves to consequate or reinforce appropriate monitoring behavior. As the client assumes independent self responsibility for each of the above activities (signalling and initiating stutter free speech, evaluating, reinforcing, and contracting) he becomes ready for transfer of the new speech response to the non-clinical environment.

Expanding Contract Activities

Environmental contract activity usually begins with three brief contracts, one in the morning, one in the afternoon, and one in the evening. The client designs these contracts so that his own comfort level is maintained and so that he feels certain that he will not experience difficulty maintaining appropriate focus on his behavior plan. Each day the client continues to increase the various parameters of the contract, including the duration of the speech act, variety of audiences, situations, excitement level, and depth of verbal content. It is important for the client to always design the increased complexity of the contract activity with his own comfort level in mind. As he accumulates more and more successful speaking experiences, communicative interactions that once seemed impossible to the stutterer become part of his reality as he becomes stutter-free. After the client is contracting between 10 to 15 contracts per day, the contract system and recording form become cumbersome. Therefore, the client may choose to use time block contracting. In this case he may use his new speech for a specific hour in the morning, afternoon, and evening, increasing the time blocks each day. The client tracks his increasing behavioral commitment on the time block contract form shown in Figure

6.2 (pp. 93–94). Each morning he decides to monitor his stutter-free speech for specific periods during the day and indicates them on his recording form. At the end of the day, he summarizes his performance and evaluates his behavior by discussing the day's activity on a tape recorder or by making a written entry into a diary. These evaluations are brought to the clinician at each therapy session. Should problems occur during the contract phase of treatment, the contract plans and client evaluations become invaluable to the client and clinician as branching steps to the program or other problem-solving strategies are devised. The environmental contract activity continues until the client is emitting monitored stutter-free speech throughout most of his entire talking day; until he has successfully completed any type of speaking situation he may have previously feared or avoided.

Schedule

During the first two phases of the program, the client must commit himself to no less than a 1-hour therapy session per day. We have found that daily therapy is necessary for the client to adequately learn the new motor programming behavior. During these initial periods, the therapeutic client–clinician relationship also begins to develop. This relationship becomes very important during the transfer phase of therapy because we believe that, based on the trust in the therapist, the client will become willing to risk transferring his new behaviors independently in his own environment. It is important that the therapist facilitates and encourages the client's independent self growth and self responsibility. Thus, the strength of the client–clinician relationship is of paramount importance to the transfer process, although growing dependence on the therapist could harm the client's favorable prognosis for success. To help the client achieve greater independence, we begin to fade the therapy session schedule on a gradual but consistent basis. He moves from everyday to three times per week, to twice a week, once a week, once every two weeks, and once a month. Although time in the formal clinical setting is being reduced, the amount of monitoring of stutter-free speech in the client's day is increasing. During the first two phases of therapy, the client produces one continuous hour of stutter-free speech daily. Once Phase III begins, the hour of daily stutter-free talking time must be maintained and increased. The therapy schedule should not be reduced until the client is able to produce more stutter-free talking time within his environment than he was previously producing in the clinic. Therefore, even though he may be contracting in the environment for short periods of time, he maintains total monitoring time with private practicing sessions alone, if need be, so that he does not reduce the total time he is under therapeutic contingencies. This is done partly to sustain his motivation, to maintain a sharp definition of his target responses, and to sustain therapy at a high attention level.

External Support System

From the literature on self-regulatory therapies and self-management therapies, we have found that some people require a great deal of external support while others thrive on independent self reinforcement. The high self-reinforcer, or one who sees himself as in control of his environment, usually transfers his new speaking behaviors easily by developing his own transfer scheme. The low self-reinforcer, or one who sees himself as the helpless victim of his environment, usually experiences difficulty in this phase of treatment. Due to his low self concept, it is difficult for him to believe that he is capable of successfully resolving so difficult and monumental a problem as his speech. Furthermore, for years he has felt victimized by his speech, and for him to assume control over the problem runs contrary to his basic belief system. Thus, in order to successfully generalize his new speech, he must change some of the basic beliefs he has about himself. This type of very personal change can create a great deal of inner turmoil and self questioning. During this period, external support systems may be necessary to help the low self-reinforcer develop his own transfer plan.

Clinical Support Systems

Group Therapy

Often during the third phase of therapy, the clients are given a weekly group session in addition to their individual appointments. The goal of the group session is to provide the client with the opportunity to learn

Clients in a group therapy session discuss contract activities.

how other clients have resolved various problems and to discuss current ones. These sessions not only provide the client with external support from other clients, but also help him understand his own problem and coping strategies more clearly. He receives group members' reactions to his own transfer scheme and possible problems, and he actively participates in helping other clients with their problems. This group problem-solving effort strengthens the client's ability to objectively design his own therapy program. Because he experiences assistance from the other group members he may more easily accept his own success in assuming control over his speech and his environment.

The Buddy System

For some clients the shift from the clinical to the non-clinical environment can be frightening. The client becomes anxious about his ability to succeed, and worries about how his new speech affects the listener. To provide some external support without creating an artificial transfer situation, clients may be assigned as buddies. Two clients would prepare, execute, and evaluate contract plans together. This type of gentle external support aids the client in his first transfer activities. Based on successful completion of these experiences, the client is better able to address independent transfer plans.

Nonclinical Support Systems

Occasionally, a client will decide to target someone in his environment as an intervention aide. This significant person may be a parent, spouse, friend, or sibling. The client may elect to bring this other person to the clinic where he can explain the goals and direction of his treatment, and his plan for including her as a part of his therapy program. For example, the client may decide to monitor his new speech anytime he speaks to the other person. By overtly committing himself to this plan and by designing it himself, the probability of the client's success is increased.

Although the therapist may be able to recognize high and low self-reinforcers, it is better to follow the direction of therapy planned by the client. If the clinician suggests the external support system idea independently, the plan might be met with a great deal of resistance and hostility; or worse, the client may agree to involve his environment in certain ways and then subconsciously sabotage the plan. Once the client begins to associate failure with his new speech, the therapeutic problems are greatly increased. One caveat that we should be aware of is the caution of inviting someone else into your therapy session. The client could easily interpret this as a violation of his relationship with the therapist and he may not wish to share this particular period of time with anyone but the therapist.

Expansion of contract transfer activities and the continuation of Phase III eventually blend into Phase IV when the client starts to progressively replace his monitored stutter-free speech with unmonitored stutter-free speech. The process is analogous to the expansion and contraction of an accordion. At first the accordion expands with increasing amounts of monitored stutter-free talking, via the transfer contract. Then at a certain point the accordion is squeezed together as monitored stutter-free speech is replaced by unmonitored stutter-free speech.

Four types of observations signal that the client is ready for the replacement process of Phase IV. These are:

1. He is monitoring easily during his entire talking day.

2. His unmonitored talking that he schedules as a reinforcer is always stutter-free.

3. His unscheduled unmonitored talking is generally stutter-free.

4. His scheduled unmonitored speech and his monitored speech sound similar in terms of rate and continuous phonation to the extent that the clinician cannot differentiate the scheduled unmonitored and monitored speech.

Some clients meet all four criteria for entering Phase IV. However, some clients never reach the point where they monitor their entire talking day. For these clients, the latter three criteria are valid for terminating Phase III and starting Phase IV.

Child Program

Clinical Contract Acitivity

Once the child is able to assume independent responsibility for his own speech behavior he is ready to begin the transfer process. In the clinic before the home transfer program is designed, the group of children and therapist design some speaking activities where each child will be responsible for instructing, monitoring, evaluating, and reinforcing his own speech responses. The therapist and children attempt to arrange a series of communicative interactions in a hierarchy ranging from those where the children should easily be able to concentrate on the new speech behaviors to more complex speaking situations. For example, a simple speech situation might be playing a game where simple verbal responses were required from each child, while making a puppet show could be more difficult, creating a play on videotape more complex, and talking to strangers even more difficult. These speech activities are then attempted in the clinic where the therapist can follow each child's ability to produce stutter-free speech. When such variables as situational complexity, excitement level, and audience are introduced into the speaking situation, the therapist reassumes certain elements of the self reinforcement paradigm. For example, the therapist evaluates and consequates the child's ability to maintain his good speech responses as excitement level or audience size changes. Then the therapist gradually turns the responsibility back to the child for these elements of the self reinforcement paradigm. This pattern repeats itself each time the situation changes. Ultimately, the child should be able to produce stutter-free speech independently without support in terms of instructive stimulus cues, evaluatory remarks, or application of consequent behaviors by the therapist over a broad range of situations in the clinic. During these activities the children are still on a point or a chip system of reinforcement.

The Parent Program

Early in Phase III of the Child Stuttering Program, the parents are brought into the treatment session. Until this time the parents have been meeting in a parent training–counseling group with a therapist while the children have been completing Phase II of therapy with another therapist. The parents have been given the opportunity to express and discuss their feelings about their children's problems, current coping, problem solving strategies for resolving them, and the impact of the problems on the child's social, academic, and home environments. Within this client-centered group framework, the therapist also serves somewhat of a didactic role. She provides information about the therapy program and helps prepare the parents for assuming responsibility for the home transfer component. For example, it is significantly important for the parents and therapists to discuss the daily routine of the child because it is within this routine that transfer of training begins.

The parent and child design home transfer contracts.

When the child is able to monitor his new speech independently, the parents are brought into the treatment session one by one. The child is given the opportunity to teach his parent the elements of the self reinforcement paradigm. The parent and child then meet with the therapist to create the home transfer program. At this time two major aspects of the program must be designed: 1) the transfer situations, and 2) the reinforcement system.

The Transfer Situations

Initially we refer to the transfer situations as *quiet times.* The parent and child agree on a time of day when they can be alone together for speech transfer activity. During this quiet time the child is required to use his new speech that is reinforced in accordance with a predetermined system. The parent and child may elect to replicate activities similar to those from the therapy sessions. For example, they may play card games or describe pictures in books or magazines. This type of activity can be highly structured, making it very easy for the parent to provide reinforcement. As the parent and child begin to feel at ease in attempting quiet times, they generally progress to more spontaneous speaking activities. For example, the child may tell his mother about his day at school or relate other activities in story fashion. Usually, the first quiet times have been either shortly after the child returns from school, at bath, or at bed time. Once the quiet times become a successful, established part of the child's day, the parent, child, and therapist begin to develop a contract plan. This contract activity, in principle, models the basic program closely. The parent,

Children begin transfer of new speech skills in the clinic

child, and therapist discuss how the child can expand the use of his new speech in more and more speaking situations. Usually the child begins by increasing the use of his stutter-free speech behavior within the home environment. If the child began quiet times with the mother, he might replicate these kinds of activities with the father and/or siblings. Later, playmates and relatives are included as duration of new speech behavior is increased concomitantly. For many children, transferring the new speaking behavior to the school environment can be a big step. If at all possible, include the school speech therapist and classroom teacher directly in the therapy program, but only when the child is ready.

The teacher and/or therapist provide reinforcement for the new speech behavior within the school setting. Thus, the child has external support systems at home, at school, and in the speech clinic. Nearly all the child's talking time comes under the stutter-free speech contingencies. As the home and school programs become effective and as the child's new speech behavior begins to stabilize, the child therapy appointments at the speech clinic are systematically decreased.

The Reinforcement System

Very early in the overall program, the concept of a reinforcement system is explained to the parents. The children are initially reinforced on a continuous schedule for each correct behavior emitted so that they learn the reinforcement system empirically and very quickly. When the child begins to transfer his new speech environmentally the parents play an extremely important role in the design and implementation of the reinforcement system. During the first parent, child, and therapist meeting, a hierarchy of back-up tangible reinforcers such as toys, games, or privileges is established. Child and parent assign token values for each item. Then the child begins to earn tokens during his quiet times that he is able to exchange for the back-up reinforcers. Throughout these activities verbal approval is also provided. This form of reinforcement eventually replaces the tangible reinforcers that are gradually faded out. As the transfer activities are expanded, the schedule for clinical sessions is gradually decreased from four times a week to three, to two, to once a week or less, depending on the child's progress.

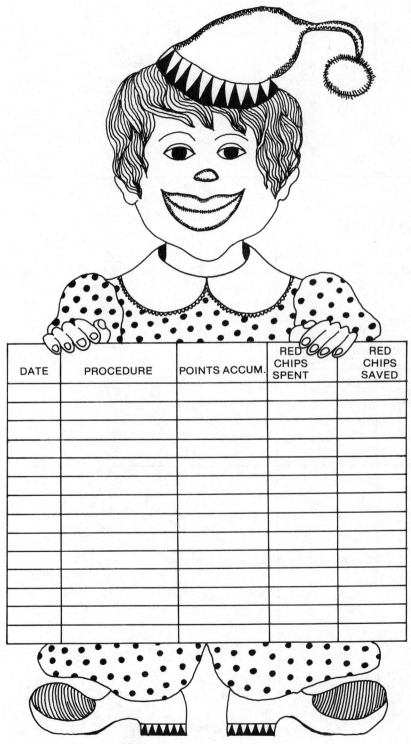

DATE	PROCEDURE	POINTS ACCUM.	RED CHIPS SPENT	RED CHIPS SAVED

Figure   6.3   *Phase III   Child Program*

DAY						
TIME						
PERSON						
PLACE						
SPEECH						

Figure 6.4 *Child Program*

DAY	TUESDAY 8-7	WEDNESDAY 8-8			
TIME	AFTER LUNCH	AFTER LUNCH / BEFORE BED			
PERSON	DAD	DAD / JANE			
PLACE	BACK YARD	BACK YARD / HOME			
SPEECH	Slow ☆ / Smooth ★	Slow ☆ / Smooth ★★			

Figure   6.5   *Sample Diary of Contract Activities*

James Gilbert-Age 52 (Severe stutterer)
Business Executive-President of Electrical Contracting Co.
Environmental Contract Activity

GILBERT CONTRACT

5/12   Telephone conversation-Milton Daniels
        Meeting-Mellon Sturat
        Dinner-Evening

5/13   Meeting with Insurance Adjuster
        Conversation with Roy Gavert-wedding
        Dinner at PFC-wedding

5/14   Conversation going to church Sunday
        Conversation with Kay during golf
        Conversation at dinner with family

5/15   Telephone call in morning with Gannon
        Lunch with employees
        Doctor's appointment with Dr. Kirk

5/16   Luncheon with office employees
        Meeting at Mercy Hospital-Mike
        Conversation with FA at home-evening

5/17   Meeting at Childrens Hospital-Architect
        Lunch with Ralph Torrence
        Dinner at PFC with John Campbell

5/18   Luncheon with office employees
        Telephone conversation-Whitney Snyder
        Discussion with Dewey

5/19   Job site meeting at PPG
        Discussion with Evan White
        Birthday party-wife

5/20   Telephone conversation with Evan White
        Company discussion with Ray
        Discussion with Al Johnson

5/21   Golf date with Rudert
        Discussion with Dewey-body work
        Dinner party-spare room

5/22   Conversation on way to church
         Golf date with wife
         Telephone conversation–Jim Malone

5/23   Conference at Hussey
              "   " SVH
         Conversation with Ray Thompson

Take 2 contracts/each time of day till 5/31—then add 1 to each period.

5/26   Ralph Altman–telephone conversation
         Jim Bragg–bid delivery to Hussey
         Dr. Hilger–conversation at office
         Dewey–discussion about car
         Dinner at home
         Conversation with Kay at home

5/27   Meeting at SVH
         Pension meeting at Lot #5
         Conversation with Lou about Kane
         Telephone conversation with Seymor
         Conversation with son, John
         Dinner at PFC with Peters. et al

5/28   Conversation with Dave Peters
         Meeting with Courtney & Johnson
         Lunch with Herman Seigel
         Conversation with Pingree relative homes
         Dinner at home
         Conversation with Dave Connelly

5/29   Morning golf game
         Men's grill conversation
         Beer distributor
         Son, Jim, conversation
         Ride to Mt. Lebanon with Kay
         Picnic at Mikus

5/30   Golf match at PFC–Memorial Day event
         Men's Grill conversation
         Conversation with neighbor
         Conversation with Roy
         Dinner at Shermans
         Conversation with Cromer

5/31   Telephone call to Whitney Snyder
         Call to Dr. Kirk
         Discussion with Jim G.
         Conversation with Ray Thompson
         Visit to 3 Rivers Festival
         Conversation with Geo. Berwanger

6/1   Telephone call with Bill Torbert
        Telephone call with Ray Thompson
        Job site meeting with Rodden
        Job site meeting with Anderson
        Conversation with son, Jim
        Conversation with Kay at home

6/2   Conversation with son John, morning
        Telephone call to Bill Torbert
        Lunch with Lee Ahearn
        Meeting at Mercy Hospital
        Telephone call to Charlie Shavers
        Dinner at home

6/3   Telephone call to Dave Peters
        Telephone call to Herb Fetzer
        Conversation with Herman Seigel
        Conversation with Ray Bayer
        Drive with wife to Washington
        Registration at motel

6/4   Breakfast with Kay
        Conversation with Johnson Family
        Wedding at Church
        Reception at Sade home
        Conversation with Mr. Sade
        Dinner with Johnsons

6/5   Breakfast with Kay
        Checkout at motel
        Conversation with wife on drive home
        Telephone call to Ray Bayer
        Conversation with children

6/6   Conversation with Dr. Shames
            "   with Bill Hayduk
            "   with Don Pegher
        Golf at St. Clair C.C.
        Cocktail hour at St. Clair
        Dinner conversation at table

6/7   Meeting at PPG
        Conversation with D. Pingree
            "   with D. Pegher
        Lunch with employees
        Conversation with Evon While
        Dinner at home

6/8   Conversation with Andy Johnson
          "   with Dr. Hilger
          Lunch at PFC
          Golf with Don Spaulding, et al.
          Conversation with Frank
          Dinner with Spaulding

6/9   Meeting with Bill Torbert
          Conversation with Steve Flaherty
          Lunch–Park Schenley–Balmet
          Meeting Mercy Hospital–M.S.
          Conversation with Ray Bayer
          Dinner at home

6/10   Call to Margaret at NECA
          Telephone conversation with Bill Wade
          "   "   with Geo. Berwanger
          Lunch at PFC
          Golf at PFC
          Dinner with A. Johnson

6/11   Golf game in morning
          Conversation with Kay on way to V.B.
          Golf game at V.B.
          Dinner
          Conversation with Shermans
          Conversation with Kay on drive home

6/12   Drive to church with family
          Breakfast at home
          Conversation with Mother
          Lunch at home
          Conversation with sons
          Dinner at home

6/13   Drive to work with son, Jim
          Meeting with Dr. Shames
          "   " Dr. Kirk
          "   " WTAE & Gambel
          "   " Evan While
          Conversation with Rudy Krall
          Dinner at home

Generalization

The transfer program continues until the child, parent, therapist, and teacher or school therapist no longer see the child as a stutterer. Usually, generalization of stutter-free speech to all speaking situations occurs during the transfer program without a great deal of ambient difficulty. When all the intervention aides agree that the problem no longer exists, formal treatment is discontinued. To date, Phase IV has never been formally implemented for the children, as it has not been necessary. Generalization of monitored stutter-free speech to automatic unmonitored speech has occurred without actual direct training. This automatic generalization observed in children may be due to the age of the child and the fact that he does not have the reinforcement history and ingrained self concept associated with his stuttering that the adult has. Therefore, the generalization process is usually completed easily.

Following completion of Phase III, the children are enrolled in the 5-year follow-up evaluation program (Phase V).

Conclusion

The majority of problems experienced by clients in this treatment program occur during the third phase of therapy. It is during this phase that the client must really come to grips with the meaning of his speech change to his life. Often these potential life changes can provoke extreme anxiety. The client may resist these changes by subconsciously undermining his own generalization plan. The following section describes some of the individual issues we have encountered during this phase of the therapy.

WHAT IF MY STUTTERER . . .

Forgets to signal?

Many clients attempt to monitor by merely thinking of continuous phonation as they produce automatic speech. The client may begin by self-instructing continuous phonation but before long he becomes involved in the content of the speech act and forgets about monitoring until he stutters. Monitoring then may become a technique for eliminating stuttering; because the client is so far from his original behavior plan by this time he may have overloaded the motor system with several plans at once. Generally, the client believes that he should be able to open his mouth and talk fluently without doing anything special about programming his speech. He resents signalling and monitoring according to a specified schedule. By this time the odds are in his favor. He is probably experiencing a large amount of coincidental fluency so that his old stuttering behaviors are occurring much less frequently. Therefore, he can gamble that for probably 80 to 90% of the time he will speak fluently without monitoring. The specific behavior plan involved in monitoring requires a great deal of concentration and commitment to total change. The client's fear of change and the chances for non-monitored fluency can often lead the client to reject the signal. However, the signal is the overt symbol of the client's commitment to his behavior plan. When he signals, he self-instructs his motor programmer to activate certain physiological responses and behaviors. When the client is monitoring correctly he is in control of his speech and he will not stutter; when he forgets to signal by definition, he also forgets to self-instruct. When he leaves his motor speech behavior to chance, he gives up overt control of his speech and he leaves the presence or absence of stuttering to chance as well. This element of chance or uncertainty leads to anxiety and anticipation of the new stuttering behavior. Thus, before long the client is in trouble. Forgetting to signal is a danger sign that indicates the client is forgetting to monitor properly. Under these circumstances, the clinician should ask the stutterer about his signalling behavior. She may even back up to a point where she provides the signal and gradually turns the responsibility for signalling back to the stutterer. In a sense, the clinician signals the stutterer to signal himself and in turn reinforces the stutterer's signalling behavior with a head nod of approval.

Wants to monitor all the time without a contract?

Difficulties occur when the client resists contracting in general. Often, a client will state that he does not need to use contracts because he will just monitor all the time. The client is learning a new motor speech response and as the response is conditioned it becomes stronger and stronger. The new speech response is not yet strong enough for the client to monitor all day. Although his intentions may be good he often ends up not monitoring correctly and fails to satisfy his goal. He usually will explore his choices, the clinician's admonitions notwithstanding. Therefore, it is felt that the clinician should permit the stutterer to explore his preference and later deal with the consequences and meaning of the stutterer's activities.

Tracks stuttering?

A second danger signal may be noted in the client's self evaluation methodology. The client may design and implement his behavior plan correctly, but when he evaluates his performance he says "I did well, I didn't stutter." In this case the client is attempting to perform in certain ways to avoid stuttering. As a result, the best therapy outcome he will ever be able to achieve will be a fluent stutterer, for he will always be waiting for the instance of stuttering to occur so that he can apply his stuttering avoidance techniques. If the client settles for the goal of being a fluent stutterer, he may be able to externally present himself to others within his environment as a fluent speaker, but internally he will see himself as someone who must do special things in order to speak correctly. Furthermore, the element of uncertainty will remain, causing the client to continue to fear a variety of speaking situations. If the client concentrates on tracking and evaluating stuttering, he is going toward the goal of becoming a fluent stutterer. If he tracks and evaluates the behavioral characteristics of normal speech—continuous phonation, prosody, and rate—he is going toward the goal of becoming a normal speaker. If this problem occurs, the clinician should explain these consequences of this choice. If the stutterer decides to go on toward the two general goals of the program, he should be refocused to evaluating continuous phonation and rate control. Verbal disapproval should be provided by the clinician for evaluative comments by the stutterer that focuses on stuttering.

Increases duration of situations but doesn't vary the situations on his transfer contract?

The need for both types of progressions should be discussed with the client. Both vertical and horizontal expansion, in terms of difficulty level, as well as duration is imperative. Otherwise, there will always be situations that will remain as sources of speech anxiety and as very real reminders that the client is still a stutterer. Without pushing the client beyond his comfort level he should discuss and recognize the value of approaching rather than avoiding situations. The stutterer should come to understand his own motives, feelings, behavior, and consequences. If there are strong fears involved, sometimes these discussions might be followed up with gradual situational desensitization activities.

Resists regimenting himself and scheduling the contract?

The client may be afraid of changing the way he is, even positively. The client should start off at a minimal level of committed action and very gradually increase his commitment as he experiences his accomplishments.

Clings to his old identity by talking about his experiences as a stutterer?

The client should be encouraged to talk about why this is important so that he understands his motives and feelings, both pro and con, about giving up his stuttering problem.

Table 6.1 Summary of Steps in Phase III Basic Therapy Paradigm

Step	Training Task	Condition	Time	Target Behavior	Contingency for Off-Target Response	Reinforcement
1	Develop Transfer Contract	Writing and explaining elements of control	10–15 min.			
2	Clinic Transfer	Vary audience, speaking situation, and stress	Client determines	Signal 80% M 20% UnM	Client determines	UnM speech
3	Environmental transfer: Situational Contracts	Expand in number, terms of duration, and difficulty to 15 contracts per day	Client determines	Signal 80% M 20% UnM	Client determines Return to Step 2	UnM speech
4	Environmental transfer: Time Block Contracts	Monitor in blocks of time until entire talking day on contract	Client determines	Signal 80% M 20% UnM	Return to Step 3	UnM speech

Materials Needed:
Situational Contract Forms
Time Block Contract Forms

M   monitored speech
UnM unmonitored speech
R   response
rf reinforcement

Table 6.2 Summary of Steps in Phase III Child Therapy Paradigm

Step	Training Task	Condition	Time	Target Behavior	Contingency for Off-Target Response	Reinforcement
1	Develop transfer contracts with therapist	Commitment to use smooth speech in clinic situation	Client and therapist determine	Smooth speech	Return to Phase II or re-evaluate contract	1 chip per phrase
2	Develop contracts with parent	Commitment to use smooth speech in home quiet times	Client, therapist, and parent determine	Smooth speech	Re-evaluate contract	1 chip per phrase
3	Develop contracts with school therapist teacher	Commitment to use smooth speech at school	Client, therapist, and teacher determine	Smooth speech	Re-evaluate contract	1 chip per phrase
4	Generalized transfer of behavior	Contracting continues until smooth speech becomes automatic	Client, therapist, and teacher determine	Smooth speech	Re-evaluate contract	1 chip per phrase

Materials Needed:
Situational Contracts
% of goal forms

Chapter 7

Phase IV   Training in Unmonitored Speech

Introduction

There are several criteria employed for starting a client into Phase IV of the therapy. The most significant criterion is that the client is able to monitor her stutter-free speech for her entire talking day and in a wide variety of speaking situations. However, in the absence of this criterion, if the client's monitored and unmonitored speech sounds the same and if both are generally free of stuttering, these are also signs that Phase IV can be initiated. Monitoring rate and continuous phonation is indeed a very special way of talking. The client has learned to volitionally program certain elements of the motor-speech act at will. Although the client is consistently producing stutter-free normal-sounding speech at this point, she is still paying special attention to the way she speaks. The goal of Phase IV is to replace these special monitoring behaviors with automatic stutter-free talking.

The Therapy Plan

At the end of the third phase of treatment, the client is using a behavior plan in which she monitors (is deliberate and concentrates on how she talks) 80% of the time and uses unmonitored speech (lets go of her concentration) for about 20% of the time as a reinforcer for monitoring. Thus, she begins a speech act with careful, deliberate concentration on monitoring the rate, continuous phonation, and forward movement of her speech. Then, either toward the end of the speech act or at various times while she is talking, she signals herself to let the words come out automatically. So during the beginning of her speech response, she pays careful attention to volitionally controlling elements of her motor programming system and relaxes the intensity of her concentration on a few words while she is talking, usually at the end of her speech act or semantic-thought unit. The paradigm for the monitored–unmonitored speech pairing is based in part on the findings of David Premack (1959). Premack found that high frequency behavior if made contingent on low frequency behavior can reinforce low frequency behavior. By definition, reinforcement increases the probability of the future occurrence of a specific response. Thus, in accordance with the Premack Principle, unmonitored speech was originally used to reinforce monitored speech in this therapy program. However, this high frequency behavior is also consistently reinforced by the client and by society; this may be the reason that the client consistently emits those behaviors. The basic reason for replacing monitored with unmonitored speech is knowing that unmonitored stutter-free speech will be reinforced by society and by the stutterer herself.

Because of its prior function during Phases II and III as a self-reinforcer under the scheduled control of the stutterer, and because it is desired by her and has a public representation, unmonitored talking has a good probability for replacing monitored speech. Its scheduled and unscheduled occurrence is already a part of the client's experience. During Phase I and Phase II, we arranged the client's responses so that she produced monitored stutter-free speech. This is a complex of behaviors under stimulus control (self instruction) that were directly adjacent to the response of a few words of automatic talking (the client's highly desired speech behavior). At that time this unmonitored stutter-free talking was used as a reinforcer for learning to program correct rate, phonation, and forward movement of motor speech behavior.

The clients discuss replacement schedules for expanding unmonitored stutter-free speech in a group setting.

Because the monitored–unmonitored paradigm is included early in the general therapy plan, there is a base of experience for the goal of Phase IV. In Phase IV we are ready to alter the learning format so that automatic talking begins to replace monitored speech. The client moves from a schedule of monitored talking 80% of the time and unmonitored talking 20% of the time to a schedule of 50% unmonitored talking, by monitoring *every other phrase.* She then reduces her monitoring further by monitoring just the *initial portion of each speech act or phrase* and using unmonitored speech for the rest. She may then monitor just the *initial portion of every other speech act or phrase.* At this point the replacement schedules become highly individualized. We have to keep in mind what the individual is capable of remembering and doing. She may move to a time-block schedule and monitor the first speech act she produces every half-hour, then every hour, and then once in the morning, afternoon, and evening. She might choose to monitor once a day, once a week, or only on payday. At this time, monitored speech may be totally replaced or the client may still elect to monitor her speech only during special events, like being on television, asking for a raise, or speaking before a large group. However, it seems that under those conditions, the normal speaker would also pay special attention to her speech; the stutterer's monitoring at special times is similar in form and intervention to the speech monitoring of non-stutterers.

High and Low Self-Reinforcers

Planning and implementing the schedule for replacing monitored with unmonitored talking varies a great deal among clients. High self-reinforcers tend to develop and carry out an appropriate, efficient, personalized replacement scheme for completing the program, making completing therapy relatively easy. The client may follow a plan similar to the one previously described. As she is working almost independently by this time, the therapy schedule is reduced from two sessions per week, to one session per week, to once every two weeks, to once a month. Usually each week the schedule is reduced, and by the time the client achieves the once a month schedule she will be ready to enter the follow-up program. The high self-reinforcer is usually fairly accurate in selecting appropriate goals and estimating her rate of change. She may use the time block form or percent of goal form (see Figure 6.1, pp. 93–94) to track and evaluate her performance. She can reinforce herself for achieving her goals and completing therapy without ambient difficulty.

The low self-reinforcer may experience a number of problems in completing Phase IV. She may need a considerable amount of planning and support in order to reach her goals. The following section lists some of the problems we have encountered, especially with low-reinforcers.

Children tend to generalize to unmonitored stutter-free speech automatically.

WHAT IF MY STUTTERER . . .

Designs an inappropriate plan?

The low self-reinforcer tends to see herself as the unfortunate victim of fate. She expects herself to fail, especially where her speech is concerned. Therefore, she often designs inappropriate therapy plans. She may attempt to set herself up for failure so that she behaves congruently with her self expectations or she may not be able to estimate her own behavior change parameters. In any case, many times the low self-reinforcer designs a plan that does not appear to be a sensible one. Often she plans to undertake too large a change too quickly or she makes very minimal changes in order to maintain a status quo for several days or weeks. At this point, the therapist must decide what his role is in the therapy process. He may choose to intervene by advising the client how she can develop a more appropriate plan; or he may choose only to follow the client as she learns from her own mistakes. We have found that a combination of these two clinician strategies works best. The clinician himself has a set of beliefs concerning what the client should be doing. They are based on the successes and failures of previous clients and his clinical experiences in general. However, it is difficult to know for sure whether or not the client's plan is going to be successful. The clinician is primarily a facilitator who helps the client resolve her own problems. Thus, in a client-centered way, the clinician should guide the client to the implementation of the best possible behavior plan without taking away the client's responsibility for her own decisions and personal growth. In this way, the client might make mistakes, but with the clinician's help she will learn to re-evaluate her plan in conjunction with her performance until an appropriate Phase IV strategy is produced.

Rejects unmonitored talking?

Changing from stuttering to monitored stutter-free speech has been a big step for many clients. As the client nears completion of Phase III, she realizes that she has sytematically trained herself to volitionally control her motor speech behavior. This sense of control over her speech may give her a sense of control over her general interactions with her environment. Monitoring her speech may have been very reinforcing; she might feel very safe when using monitored speech. The results of her experiences have conditioned her to believe that she will not stutter when she monitors and that she can depend on speaking in a specific way when she self-instructs certain behaviors. Therefore, she may be reluctant or afraid to give up volitionally controlled speech. Automatic unmonitored speech can be frightening. The client might fear that her stuttering will return or she might fear becoming a normal speaker. As long as she monitors her speech, she continues to regard herself as someone who does something special when she talks. Thus, as long as she believes that monitoring is necessary for stutter-free speech, she can maintain the self concept of an abnormal speaker. Because of her speaking differences, she can continue to avoid situations and people as her primary coping mechanism, even though she presents no stuttering behaviors overtly. As a result she appears to be a normal speaker to the outside world, but inside she still sees herself as someone behaving in special ways to prevent stuttering. In response to the fear of changing her self concept or the safety that comes from assuming volitional control over the problem, the client may resist changing to unmonitored automatic talking. She might reject treatment plans suggested by the therapist. She might subconsciously sabotage her own treatment plan so that she cannot succeed. She might propose dismissing herself from therapy, optimistically expecting to complete the program on her own; or she might insist that she needs to remain in Phase III for a longer time. Any of these feelings and beliefs are important for the client and clinician to probe and analyze so that the client can achieve permanent and durable changes in her speech and, hopefully in her self concept. The client is nearing completion of treatment; when she accepts moving into unmonitored speech she is actually committing herself to becoming a normal speaker. For a time, the replacement process may have to be delayed until the client and clinician discuss and understand and, if necessary, renegotiate this goal of therapy. How far she goes with the therapy is ultimately the client's decision.

Resists terminating the therapeutic relationship?

As the client progresses through therapy, she begins to value the quality of the therapeutic relationship. The clinician has given his undivided attention to the client focusing on her problems, her treatment strategies, and her future plans. His intense attention to the client's needs has given the client a sense of importance, a belief in her own worth. The kind of trust, understanding, and empathy that the client feels comes from this unique one-sided type of relationship where the clinician subordinates his needs to the wellbeing of the client. All energies from both parties are directed toward solving the client's problem. This type of relationship is not found in general everyday living. In the parent–child, peer, or marital relationship, needs from both parties are recognized and handled. Compromising, sharing, a general give and take between people develops. But in the therapeutic relationship, the focus remains entirely on the client. As discussed in Chapter 2, Strupp believes that in therapy the client continues to test the validity of the therapeutic relationship until she capitulates and submits to the honesty of the therapist's intentions, until she can trust the therapist's commitment to her own well-being. When the client reaches this point she will change out of love for her therapist. Many of these feelings on the part of the client come together in Phase IV. The client really faces completing therapy and making a total and permanent change in her speech. The therapist has helped the client facilitate these changes but he has also given the client a very unique, warm, and nurturing environment for personal self exploration and growth. Many clients find it difficult to give up the therapeutic relationship and return to a seemingly uncaring, unsupportive world. These clients fear their growing independence and have trouble breaking away from the client–clinician bond. Such issues in the relationship are made manifest when the client has difficulty replacing monitored speech with automatic stutter-free speech.

To help the client get ready for termination of therapy, we explain from the outset that the treatment schedule will be systematically faded week by week. Thus, the client does not have to make an abrupt break from an intensive schedule and adjusts to her emerging independence gradually. Nevertheless, many clients will impede their own progress to avoid losing the therapeutic relationship. Furthermore, the client may try to change the relationship so that she can complete therapy and still maintain some kind of relationship with the therapist. For example, the client might invite the therapist to social functions. She might ask him to her home as a guest or assist him in other projects. It is important that the client and clinician explore and discuss their relationship tactfully, especially when problems related to termination arise.

Clients who seem to have difficulty with termination can be asked if they would be willing to return to help other clients who might be struggling with a particular portion of treatment. They can be asked if they would be willing to speak at a clinician-training seminar. In addition, all clients are contacted yearly for a 5-year period as part of their follow-up program. The client's awareness of this type of future contact with the therapist allows her to feel that she has not been cut off completely from the clinic. At the same time, this future plan keeps the therapist's role in the client's life in appropriate perspective.

Gambles on the low probability of stuttering?

By the time the client reaches Phase IV, the chances that stuttering will occur are minimal. Usually, the client feels good about her speech improvement and her growing self-confidence in controlling her speech. she knows from experience that the probabilities of her stuttering are very few. She realizes and has experienced the intense effort required to concentrate on a monitor/unmonitoring schedule. The client may often gamble that she will be fluent without doing anything special about her speech. Unfortunately, the client is usually correct in her assumption. She will be able to speak fluently, nearly all the time, without doing anything special about the way she programs her motor speech responses. However, even a 1% chance of stuttering creates a degree of uncertainty in the stutterer's mind about what will come out of her mouth. Her uncertainty leads her to fear especially in high stress situations. As a result, the client still experiences the problem of stuttering and will not be able to change her self concept.

If the client decides to gamble with Phase IV acitvities she may display various off-target behaviors. She may decide to monitor only when she is in a high stress situation or only when she thinks she might stutter. She plans to use monitoring to avoid stuttering, and has developed a scheme in which she will always be a stutterer anticipating the next breakdown. She is actually monitoring stuttering and not the behaviors she has learned to monitor in therapy. Furthermore, monitoring used to remedy stuttering usually doesn't work. By the time the stutterer is in the midst of a complex of stuttering behaviors, it is too late to try to program the self-reinforcement paradigm characteristic of monitoring stutter-free speech (rate, continued phonation and forward moving speech). The client therefore fails in her attempt to become fluent by using the monitoring "technique" that increases her anxiety, and, makes her fear the next occurrence of stuttering. She may then return to tricks she used to avoid stuttering in the past, such as forcing, word substitutions, circumlocutions and so forth. What appeared to be a sensible gamble is now beginning to change. The client's uncertainty about her control of speech increases and may lead to a higher frequency of stuttering. As a result, gambling during Phase IV activities can lead to relapse difficulties.

It is tempting for the stutterer to think of those behaviors that she monitors as fluency because they are stutter-free behaviors. However, both the clinician and the stutterer should be cautious even about using the term *fluency*. Fluency is not a behavior. It may be the result of behavior. To try to be fluent or to seek fluency is not the same as monitoring the rate of talking and continuous phonation. Confusing the two, even when we talk about it, can detract the stutterer from her focus on behavior.

Retains an incongruent self concept?

The goal of Phase IV is that the client replace monitored speech with unmonitored speech. During this phase the client really comes to grips with making a total, permanent change in her speech. What she may fear most about changing her speech behavior is the impact those changes will have on her self concept and life system in general. For example, as the client grows more independent in her problem-solving ability, as she feels more self-confident in resolving her speech problem, she may feel that she has outgrown past relationships in her life. She may see herself emerging a new person, capable of many new life experiences. Such developing self perceptions can threaten her involvement with her existing relationships. The client may feel she needs to break away from parental supervision or a domineering spouse. The client may desire to explore the wealth of new social, educational, and vocational opportunities. All of these possible changes in the client's life can be frightening and can make the completion of therapy appear to be a much bigger step than merely replacing monitored with unmonitored speech. The client–centered relationship has been developing since the first day of therapy to help the client deal with the impact of her speech change. Hopefully, as a result of the therapeutic relationship, the client has developed her ability to independently solve her own problems and recognize her own self worth. She may have developed new coping strategies and defense mechanisms so that stuttering is no longer necessary for her self protection. As the client begins to realize her own protential, based on the successful change in her speech, she will begin to see herself differently. How long does it take for human beings to change their self concepts? In the context of the stuttering problem we must pursue this question carefully. Experiencing consistent, unmonitored stutter-free talking, it may be a long time before the client begins to really understand her problem as part of the past. Our role is to be there and to be supportive when the stutterer vacillates between the old and the new, between the past and future. We serve as the stutterer's sounding board and champion for her feelings as she makes choices for herself. We help her recognize and evaluate various short-term and long-term consequences of her decisions. Although *our* goals for the stutterer are speech that is free of stuttering and a self perception as a non-stuttering speaker, the decisions and goals of therapy are ultimately the stutterer's. Whatever she chooses as her own most comfortable and happy human condition is the goal of therapy that we both share.

Relapses to her old ways of talking?

Relapse can mean many things to many people. It can mean reverting to some original status in terms of behavior, reasoning, and feelings; or it can denote a mere step back to a previous stage of therapy. Such reversions or regressions can occur at any time during any stage of therapy. Very often when there is a relapse, panic sets in for both the stutterer and the clinician; everyone begins to ask ''Where did we go wrong?''

Several issues must be resolved under such circumstances. Of course, first we must control our own panic so that we can focus on the client and her needs rather than on our own anxieties. Once that is accomplished, we should encourage the stutterer to express her panic and feelings rather than to suppress them. During these times we might touch upon some significant emotional material that would otherwise be hidden.

Finally, on a more intellectual level, we analyze what has occurred. We should acknowledge the fact that the stutterer has a large repertoire of behaviors, ideas, and feelings that have varying degrees of strength. Depending on the circumstance, some of those behaviors and ideas which have been lying dormant for a while may be expressed. Under certain stimulus conditions any part or parts of our repertoire are available for expression. This concept of stimulus control over the stutterer's behavior can be applied to problems of relapse in several ways. In this behavioral sense, relapse can be viewed as any other behavior: the emission of a response on the occasion of a particular stimulus when the contingent consequence is prepotent over all other competing stimuli, responses and consequences that could be operative at that time. What makes this a circumstance of relapse is our value judgment of it as a reversion or regression to any earlier state.

We should also acknowledge that a single response, or a group of responses that occur together, as in stuttering (motor speech, cognitive, emotional reactions) may be controlled by many different stimuli. Stimuli associated with people, talking situations, and topic of conversation, may exercise separate control as well as combined control over the emission of stuttering behaviors and reactions. Therefore, trouble shooting a relapse problem may require a thorough analysis of various elements of the behavioral paradigm.

One of the first things we need is a thorough description of the behavior under consideration, its frequency of occurrence, the occasions for its occurrence, and the consequences of its occurrence. One instance of an undesirable behavior does not constitute relapse. Of course, we must depend on the stutterer to provide this description as accurately and as detailed as possible. We should then compare her description of the relapse activity and circumstances with a description of the circumstances when she was behaving more appropriately. From this comparison we should be able to track the problem. We should be able to see where the descriptions vary from one another, in terms of:

1. The stimulus occasion.
2. The source of reinforcement.
3. The form of reinforcement.
4. The schedule of reinforcement.

We should be able to identify a regression to a particular Phase of Therapy, i.e., to a problem in the self reinforcement paradigm of:

1. Signalling or self instructing.
2. Emitting the appropriate behavior.
3. Evaluating the response.
4. Reinforcing (the use of unmonitored speech).

to response definition; to ambigous contracting activities, etc.

We should be able to determine if we have taken too big a step from where the stutterer had been successful in his therapy, to activities where he is experiencing relapse. By analyzing these factors, we should be able to revise our tactics so that the stutterer can move through her therapeutic experiences with more consistent and progressive success.

If there is a radical reversion to a pre-therapy status we may put the stutterer through an abbreviated form of the entire experience from its beginning, as a type of recapitulation and re-experiencing of a summary form of the therapy to re-establish and strengthen his pre-relapse status.

Not all stutterers successfully complete Phase IV. Some of them cling to their monitoring even for very infrequent instances, although they do not stutter. Others cling to their long standing identity as a stutterer in the absence of any overt or covert stuttering behavior. But many go the whole way and emerge from their therapy with most profound and awesome changes. In those instances, we and the stutterers have truly encountered each other in the most positive sense. The total replacement of monitored speech with unmonitored speech provides a reality base for changes in self concept.

Table 7.1 Summary of Steps in Phase IV Basic Therapy Paradigm

Step	Training Task	Condition	Time	Target Behavior	Contingency for Off-Target Response	Reinforcement
1	Replace monitored speech	Increase unmonitored speech, ratio schedule	Client determines	50 M 50 UnM per speech act	Return to 80-20	UnM
2	Replace monitored speech	increase unmonitored speech, ratio schedule	Client determines	10% M 90% UnM	Return to 50-50	UnM
3	Replace monitored speech	Time block schedule	Client determines	Begin of utterance each ½ hr.	Return to 90-10	UnM
4	Replace monitored speech	Time block schedule	Client determines	Begin of utterance each hr. M 2-3 min.	Return to Step 3	UnM
5	Replace monitored speech	Time block schedule	Client determines	Begin of utterance M once in A.M. once in early P.M., late P.M.	Return to Step 4	
6	Replace monitored speech	Time block schedule	Client determines	M once per day		
7				M special events		

M   monitored speech
UnM unmonitored speech

Materials Needed:
Contract
Time Block
% of Goal Forms
Speech Diary

Chapter
8

Phase V   Follow-Up and
Therapy Outcome Studies

Introduction

Phase V of the therapy is the follow-up stage. It is a continuation of the previous phase when the stutterer is involved in replacing his monitored speech with unmonitored speech. Phase V is considered in operation when the stutterer is attending clinical sessions once a month or less. He usually is still involved in his *replacement* activities during his follow-up studies.

The goals of this stage of therapy are to provide appropriate support for the client's continued replacement of monitored with unmonitored speech, to determine the general impact of therapy on the client's life, to determine the durability and permanence of changes observed in the client during the first four phases of his therapy, and to help the client with any problems he may be experiencing.

Follow-up studies of the long-term effects of speech therapy are perhaps the most neglected phases of professional clinical regimes. Past research designed to demonstrate the efficacy of clinical tactics in speech therapy have been notably deficient. There would be little disagreement that such follow-up studies are needed in order to understand our successes and our failures, and to improve our clinical tactics. In addition to being the subject of research, such endeavors should become a regular and systematically integrated phase of therapy programs. As our technology for changing behavior within short-term laboratory or rehabilitation clinic settings improves, we are arriving at a point where we are professionally ready to confront the problems and issues involved in follow-up case studies. Although great strides have been made in changing communication behavior, and although we have begun to confront the problem of immediate, short-term carryover of new behavior out of the clinic and into the everyday life of the client, we have little information regarding the long-term permanence of such changes and carryover and its impact on the client's life style. We do not really know if the time, effort, space, equipment, and money that have been invested in the training of clinicians, in research, and in providing clinical services have any validity in terms of permanent improvements or life impact in the speech impaired.

When we look at the spectrum of serious speech problems that may prove handicapping, we realize that follow-up studies are particularly important in those instances where new speaking skills may be minimally established in the clinic, or where these new skills depend on client self monitoring following formal clinical contact, or where real social interaction may constitute a problem in generalizing new speaking behavior. Such is the case in problems of stuttering. Most follow-up information is short-term and anecdotal. We do not know whether changes in speech are permanent. We do not know of the impact of therapy on the client's life in terms of his social and emotional behavior, occupation, family, education, and general well-being as a happy and contributing member of society. There are a number of explanations available to explain this problem. But they are explanations, not justifications. These include such issues as non-standardized measures and information about clients, problems of logistics, identification and confidentiality of individual clients, biased sampling of clients and therefore biased interpretation on a group basis.

We do know from comments by stutterers, parents, and teachers that stutterers may experience social embarrassment; avoid classroom recitation; feel that they are the target of ridicule; are frustrated at not fulfilling their educational or vocational potential; feel isolated from their peers; may have depressed affects and set lower goals (social, educational and vocational) for themselves; may have lost a sense of their own worth, value, and potential to be happy and productive human beings. Their problem has permeated their entire life and becomes the nucleus around which they focus their existence. The things that we take for granted like saying our names, using a telephone, sharing our opinions, shopping, eating in a restaurant, or asking for information are major crises for stutterers. These are the routine aspects of living that we should be probing during follow-up studies. In addition we should probe any major changes in the stutterer's life system. If a therapy has been effective, its effects should be reflected in these everyday living endeavors.

This kind of information is cumbersome, sometimes difficult to obtain and awkward to organize in research reports. It appears that individual case studies may be the most viable way to assess these life system impact factors. Eventually, perhaps enough individual case-study information can be gathered and pooled to enable large scale generalizations. But in the interim, these data should be gathered and assessed and should influence our clinical management in individual cases.

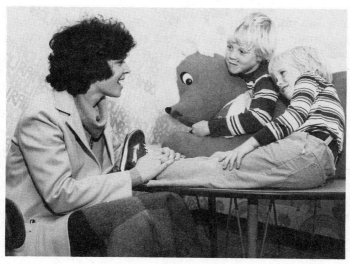

Follow-up visits are scheduled to assess durability and permanence of behavior change over a 5-year period.

Follow-up study by definition means determining the client's current status at the time of study in comparison with earlier measures or observations of the client, either pre-therapy, during therapy, or immediately following therapy. In this particular regime of therapy, a protocol of 17 measures are currently being explored on a systematic and experimental basis to determine the permanence of certain changes in speech, self concept, perceptions of others, self-reinforcing tendencies, motivation, and coping styles. In addition to this protocol of measures which is being employed on a specific time schedule, opportunity is available for comments from the client and from significant people in the client's environment to provide other information of an anecdotal nature about the client.

The 17 measures of the protocol are for your information and selective use; they may be available for your particular circumstance.

Measurements Employed on the Stutterers

Prior to entering their respective therapy programs the stutterers are individually administered the following measures:

1. Rate of speaking.
   Clinical Sample: Each stutterer engages in a brief conversation with the therapist. The sample of conversation is tape recorded and the number of words per minute during a 5-minute conversation is analyzed.
   Home Sample: A tape recording is made of each stutterer's speech in his home at the family dinner table. A sample of a minimum of 3 minutes is analyzed for words per minute.

2. Frequency of stuttering.
   Clinical Sample: The same sample of speech obtained in measurement number 1 is analyzed for number of words stuttered divided by number of words uttered.
   Home Sample: The same sample of speech obtained in measurement number 1 is analyzed for number of words stuttered divided by number of words uttered.

3. Syllable rate.
   The tape recordings obtained in measurements 1 and 2 (at home and in the clinic) are fed into a *Kay Elemetrics Visi Pitch Frequency Analyzer.* This enables an identification of number of syllables uttered divided by actual talking time, in segments of 8½ seconds duration. The entire 5-minute (clinical) and 3-minute (home) samples are analyzed, and measures of central tendency and variability are computed.

4. Continuity of phonation—tape recorded.
   The home and clinical samples of speech are analyzed for number

of breaks in phonation, both between and within phrases, by the Visi Pitch Frequency Analyzer. Measures of central tendency and variability are computed.

5. Listener judgments of differences in speech.
   Three judges are told that they will listen to a series of pairs of speakers and that one of the pair is a stutterer. Their task is to indicate which member of the pair is the stutterer. A 1-minute sample of the home sample, and a 1-minute sample of the clinical sample of the stutterer's speech is taken. Each is paired with a 1-minute sample of speech by a nonstutterer of a comparable age and sex. Percentage of correct identifications are computed, and a mean percentage for each is derived.

6. Self concept as a speaker.
   Each stutterer is asked to indicate if he thinks he:
   a. Is a stutterer
   b. Used to stutter
   c. Never stuttered

7. Teacher's report of stuttering (for school-age subjects).
   Teachers are asked to rate the severity of the stutterer's speech problem:
   a. A severe stutterer
   b. A moderate stutterer
   c. A mild stutterer
   d. Doesn't stutter

8. Parents' report of stuttering.
   Mothers and fathers are asked to rate the severity of the stutterer's speech problem:
   a. A severe stutterer
   b. A moderate stutterer
   c. A mild stutterer
   d. Doesn't stutter

9. Self report of stuttering.
   Each stutterer is asked to rate the severity of his problem:
   a. A severe stutterer
   b. A moderate stutterer
   c. A mild stutterer
   d. Doesn't stutter

10. Stutterer's assessment of seriousness of the problem.
    Each stutterer is asked to indicate the seriousness of his problem:
    a. My speech is a constant serious problem for me.
    b. My speech is frequently a problem to me.
    c. My speech is occasionally a problem for me.
    d. My speech is very infrequently a problem for me.
    e. My speech is not a problem for me.

11. Frequency of monitoring.
    Each stutterer is asked to indicate the frequency of his monitoring:
    a. A great deal
    b. Occasionally
    c. Only for special events
    d. Almost never
    e. Do not monitor at all
12. Therapist's assessment of the client's motivation to change his behavior.
    a. Highly motivated most of the time
    b. Motivation fluctuates
    c. Does not appear to be motivated
13. Parent–Child verbal interaction analysis.
    Each subject and one parent is videotaped during their initial evaluation session. The videotape is submitted to an analysis of the verbal interaction between the parent and subject using the Shames-Egolf method for evaluating parent-child verbal interactions.*
    [After the stutterer has entered his therapy programs the following measures are made.]
14. Number of phases of therapy completed.
15. Time to complete each phase in terms of number of therapy sessions.
16. Internal-External Locus of Control.
    The Rotter Measure of I-E Locus of Control is used to determine whether the stutterer feels as though he is in control of his destiny.
17. Coping styles.
    Coping is viewed within Haan's conceptualizations of coping as an ego process that is differentiated from defense mechanisms. This measure is an attempt to determine whether the therapy has had any deep psychodynamic effects on the ways in which stutterers deal with stress in their lives. A series of coping scales have been derived from the California Personality Inventory (CPI). Table 8.1 shows the series of coping scales.

The protocol shown in Table 8.2 is being used for research purposes to develop a series of standardized measures that enable pre-therapy prediction of outcome as well as short-term and long-term evaluation of the effects of therapy. However, some of these measures may be fairly easy to employ for immediate clinical use. These would include:

1. Rate of speaking (number of words spoken per minute or number of syllables per minute).

2. Frequency of stuttering (number of words stuttered/number of words uttered).

---

*See Appendix

Table 8.1 *Coping Scales*

Coping	Defense
Objectivity	Isolation
Intellectuality	Intellectualization
Logical Analysis	Rationalization
Concentration	Denial
Tolerance of Ambiguity	Doubt
Empathy	Projection
Regression-Ego	Regression
Sublimation	Displacement
Substitution	Reaction Formation
Suppression	Repression
Total Coping	Total Defense
Controlled Coping	Structured Defense
Expressive Coping	Primitive Defense

Table 8.2 shows the schedule for administering the measures.

Table 8.2 *Schedule*

Time of Measurement	Specific Measures Employed
Pre Intervention	1–10, 13
Post Phase I	1–10, 12, 15
Post Phase II	1–10, 12, 15
Post Phase III	1–12, 15, 16
Three months after Initiation of Phase I	1–12, 14, 15, 16, 17
Six months after Initiation of Phase I	1–12, 14, 15, 16, 17
12 months after Initiation of Phase I	1–15, 16, 17
18 months after Initiation of Phase I	1–15, 16, 17
24 months after Initiation of Phase I	1–17
36 months after Initiation of Phase I	1–17
48 months after Initiation of Phase I	1–17
60 months after Initiation of Phase I	1–17

3. Listeners' judgments of differences in speech.

4. Self concept as a speaker.

5. Teacher's report of stuttering.

6. Parent's report of stuttering.

7. Self report of stuttering.

8. Stutterer's assessment of seriousness of problem.

9. Stutterer's assessment of frequency of monitoring.

10. Therapist's assessment of motivation.

11. Number of phases of therapy completed.

12. Number of sessions.

One of the questions that every clinician must ask, whether it involves her current therapy or therapy that she is contemplating, is "How good it is?" We have been suggesting things that we should be assessing (speech, self perception, long term impacts on life, perceptions of others, etc.) as ways of arriving at an answer to that question. We should be sure that the things we assess and where and when we assess them provide valid, reliable, real life information. It is too easy to deceive ourselves into thinking that we have contributed to significant therapeutic change by sampling non-representative behavior, or by not following a client over a significant interval of post-therapy time.

Most of the time when we hear about or read about measures of effectiveness of therapy, the information is in the form of percentage of success. These reports are often extremely difficult to understand or to interpret.

Sometimes the criteria of success are not defined. Sometimes the criteria themselves are of questionable merit (i.e., a residual of 1% stuttering or 3% stuttering), or are too limited or narrow in scope, by relating only to overt, audible speech. Sometimes the measurements employed are of questionable validity, or are not comparable. When effectiveness is reported as a percentage of success, we have to know what goes into the numerator and what goes into the denominator.

Most recent reports about effectiveness have been less than optimistic, reporting success rates of about 50% of all who started therapy (Perkins, 1971), (Van Riper, 1973), (Martin & Ingham, 1973), (Ingham & Andrews, 1973). Many reports are concerned with the number of stuttered words in the therapy room as a therapeutic criterion as well as a measure of outcome. We must ask: "Fifty percent of what? All who completed therapy? All who at some time in therapy became fluent?" More questions we must ask are: "Success for how long? During clinical contacts? Three months after termination? One year, two years, five years? In the real life environment?" These are all reasonable questions, and they strongly suggest that "percentage of success" is too simplistic an approach to the answers we need in order to make judgments on a group basis about a therapy. It certainly is inappropriate in talking about the success of an individual client.

For these reasons, we are attempting to provide a multi-dimensional report of outcome of therapy in terms of the two basic goals of this therapy. On a quantitative basis we are assessing changes in the stutterer's speech and changes in the stutterer's perception of himself as a speaker, so we can answer two questions: "Does he still stutter?" and "Does he still think of himself as a stutterer?"

In obtaining answers to these two questions we have derived nine different categories of reasons that therapy was terminated and six different categories of outcome status of the 152 stutterers who started their therapy in this program during the last 5 years.

Table 8.3 summarizes these outcome data. As we examine the categories and data of this table, we also present illustrative case study information to both highlight and detail some of the life impact information associated with these therapy outcomes.

Table   8.3   *Therapy and Outcome Status for 152 Stutterers*

	A	B	C	D	E	F	Total
1	30	6	5	4	8	3	56
2	7	1	1	1	1	0	11
3	0	13	14	8	2	0	37
4	6	0	0	0	1	1	8
5	4	2	0	5	2	1	14
6	9	0	0	0	1	0	10
7	10	0	0	0	2	0	12
8	4	0	0	0	0	0	4
Total	70	22	20	18	17	5	152

Note: Key for Table 8.3

Reason for Termination   *Present Self Concept*

1. Still in therapy

    A. Still a stutterer

2. Moved

    B. No longer a stutterer—does not monitor

3. Strictly Follow-up
   (1 session per month or less)

    C. No longer a stutterer with occasional monitoring

4. Scheduling problems

    D. Perceived as a stutterer who speaks fluently

5. Self dismissal optimistic of change

    E. Perceived as a mild stutterer who exhibits mild stuttering

6. Self dismissal pessimistic of change

    F. Perceived as a non-stutterer who exhibits mild stuttering

7. Financial problems

8. Family and/or health problems

We can see from Table 8.3 that the data are based on 152 stutterers. The rows in the table numbered 1 through 8 represent different therapy status or termination categories. In the columns lettered A through F are different combinations of speech status and self concept status. Therefore, there are 48 different possibilities of therapy, speech, and self concept status represented in the table. The data go back over the past 5 years (1974-1979). To appreciate the intricacies and the details of these therapy outcomes we should examine this table row by row and column by column.

In Row 1, we see that 56 of the 152 stutterers are still in therapy. They are being seen more than once a month and are in one of the first four phases of therapy. Thirty-eight of these 56 still stutter and perceive themselves as stutterers, although eight of these are very mild in both self perception as well as in actual stuttering. Columns B, C, and D refer to stutterers who no longer stutter, either in the therapy sessions or in their environment. Sixty of the 152 who started therapy are in this category. Fifteen of these 60 are still in therapy even though they no longer stutter. Thirty-seven of the stutterers are in the follow-up stage of therapy. They are being seen less than once a month. Many of them are being seen once a year and range back over the past 5 years. Of the 37, 35 no longer stutter and 27 no longer perceive themselves as stutterers. Thirteen no longer engage in any special monitoring of their speech, while 14 monitor only very occasionally.

There may be ways of pooling these data and combining categories that may provide us with a justifiable quantitative measure of "percent of success." Table 8.4 attempts to provide such an assessment.

Table   8.4   *Summary Table*

	N	Categories (B, C, D) No longer Stutters	Categories (B, C, F) Self Concept of Non Stuttering
Still in Therapy	56	15	14
Premature Termination	59		
(categories 2, 4, 5, 6, 7, 8)		10	6
Follow-up	37	35	27
(Category 3)			
Total	152	60	43

Fifty-six subjects are still in therapy, 59 terminated their therapy prematurely, and 37 are in the follow-up stage.

From the pooled table given, we see that 94½% of those in follow-up status no longer stutter anywhere. Seventy-three percent of them no longer think of themselves as stutterers. It is interesting to note that of the 14 stutterers who no longer think of themselves as stutterers but are still in therapy, 11 of them do not stutter, and all were in Phase IV of the therapy program.

Although we are encouraged by these percentages of success, especially of those in the follow-up phase, we also have some concerns. Five and one-half percent of those in follow-up either still stutter occasionally and mildly or still see themselves as stutterers. The most significant result is the 73% who no longer stutter, do not monitor their speech, and do not see themselves as stutterers. An additional 21% no longer stutter, may monitor only occasionally, but still see themselves as stutterers. It appears that continued monitoring of speech gives the stutterer a reality base for retaining his self concept as a stutterer. However, our vigilance is not limited to those who are now in the follow-up stage. We are also concerned with those

56 stutterers who are still in therapy and we need to follow all of these clients for a period of 5 years. Another concern involves understanding why 59 clients, or about 38% of those who started therapy, prematurely terminated their programs. In many instances the reasons were straightforward and out of control of the stutterer and the clinician. However, in some instances the stutterers started, tried, and stopped too soon. Sometimes this occurred with great optimism about the future. In other instances the stutterer "gave up" because his progress was slow and he was having serious difficulties in one of the first four phases of therapy. We still have the task of identifying some of the less obvious reasons for these premature terminations and to try to rearrange the therapy to accomodate the particular needs of these clients. Research on this issue is currently underway with specific focus on:

1. The client's motivation and/or resistance to change
2. The client's tendencies to self-reinforce
3. The client's needs for external reinforcement and environmental support
4. An assessment of the client's psychological coping styles
5. An assessment of the client's general personality characteristics

Information about these issues will provide guidance on how to restructure the elements of their therapy, including not only the four phases of therapy that focus on speech, but also the structure and process of the clinical relationship itself.

The particular population represented in these tables is spread out over a period of 5 years, with some already having been followed for 5 years, some for 4, and some for less than a year since they entered the follow-up stage. As these data accumulate, both quantitative and anecdotal, they are being analyzed and pooled for a future research report. Currently, the most informative and descriptive way of reporting specific outcomes is through individual case studies that illustrate various issues and processes that seem to be significant for learning this particular therapy for stuttering.

CASE STUDIES

Case 1

The first case study presented is an example of a client who no longer stutters, does not monitor his speech in any special way, and does not see himself as a stutterer.

Background Information

Jack, a 24-year-old unmarried male reported that he had lived with a stuttering problem since early childhood. He stated that nearly no one other than his parents knew that he stuttered because he had become quite adept at substituting synonyms or circumlocuting when he thought he would stutter. He decided to pursue a career as an attorney, but felt that he would not be able to succeed unless he changed his speech behavior. Prior to therapy he worked as a janitor to finance law school expenses. He talked very little to avoid revealing to friends that he had a problem. At the time of his initial interview he stuttered about 7% of the time and spoke at a rate of 121 words per minute. He was rated as having a mild problem by his therapist.

Therapy Schema

Jack started therapy on a daily basis and completed each of the treatment phases quickly and without difficulty. Phase 1, Establishing Volitional Control of Speech, was completed in 2½ hours. Jack experienced no difficulty focusing on rate and phonation, and his previous stuttering behaviors of word substituting or circumlocuting dropped out completely. As he progressed through Phase 1 Jack's dialogue about himself and his world view suggested that he was a high self-reinforcer, with an internal locus of control. He reported that he believed his life reflected a series of the conscious choices and decisions he had made. A highly organized person, Jack tended to schedule a daily routine, assigning specific times for attending classes, working, studying, and playing. He generally created a list of things he hoped to accomplish each day, even on weekend days. Thus, training in self reinforcement was very easy for him. He liked the high degree of structure involved in the task. Breaking his speech response into the four elements of instruction, monitoring, evaluation, and consequation was logical to him. He was able to assume responsibility for all aspects of the self reinforcement regime in less than a half-hour time period. Before the end of the first week of therapy, Jack was ready to transfer his newly learned stutter-free speech behavior to the environment. In planning the contract activity, Jack stated that he was excited about beginning the transfer phase. He felt he did not need to practice contract activities in the clinic, and selected three contracts, one for that afternoon, one for that evening, and one for the following morning before therapy. He decided to monitor for 10 minutes of conversational speech during each contract and to signal 80% monitored speech and 20% unmonitored speech for each speech act. Jack returned the following day reporting happily that he had succeeded in regard to each dimension of his contract perfectly. Because of the general degree of high self-regulation in Jack's daily life, it was very easy for him to develop and implement a contract schedule that he systematically increased until his entire talking day was under contingencies. During the second week of his therapy, he attended three sessions; during the third week, two sessions; and by the beginning of the fourth week, he was ready to begin Phase IV. The elements of replacing monitored with unmonitored speech again appealed to Jack's high degree of structure. He systematically made a plan for replacement following a decrease in the proportionate use of monitored versus unmonitored speech, and then moving to fading the monitored speech on a time block schedule. He attended therapy twice the fourth week and one time per week for the fifth and sixth weeks. By the end of the sixth week, Jack and the therapist believed that he was ready to terminate active therapy. During his final interview no stuttering was observed and his speech rate was 160 words per minute.

Outcome and Impact of Change

Jack has been dismissed from therapy for a 2-year period. He currently does not stutter, does not produce any unnatural speaking behavior, and does not monitor his speech. He sees himself as a normal speaker. Shortly after completing therapy, he was able to competitively interview for a legal aide position, a job he still holds as he completes law school. During the diagnostic session, Jack reported that he knew that this therapy program was appropriate for resolving his problem. He seemed to completely embrace the system, the therapist, and the therapy activities without any doubt, resistance, or questions. It was important for him to thoroughly understand the rationale for each stage of therapy. But once explained to him, he seemed to feel that the steps and phases were logical, well planned, and adequately supported by research findings. Therefore, he seemed to follow the therapy program rigorously but not blindly without analyzing carefully what he was doing. Interestingly enough, he reported a total change in self concept shortly after the 6-week therapy program. He feels that his speech problem is completely a part of his past and has no fear of relapse.

Case 2

The second case study is an illustration of a client who no longer stutters, does not moniter her speech in any way, but still retains her self concept of a stutterer.

Background Information

Dorothy, a 35-year-old unmarried female came to the clinic on the recommendation of her vocational supervisor. She was given a leave of absence from her job to correct her speech disorder. Her employer had read about this therapy program and was very enthusiastic about the program's potential for helping Dorothy. Dorothy, on the other hand, basically felt that her problem could not be helped. She believed that it was God's will that she live her life as a stutterer so that she would understand the pain of those less fortunate than her. She had been enrolled in public school speech therapy throughout her elementary and high school years. However, in therapy she had been told repeatedly that stuttering was a problem that could not be changed and that she must accept the problem and learn to live with it as happily as she could. None of her previous therapy was designed to reduce the frequency of her stuttering. As a child she had been included in group articulation therapy. The other children were learning to produce accurate articulation behaviors while she was simply required to speak and feel comfortable from time to time whenever the public school therapist could manage to see her. In these sessions, she was counseled to accept her handicap and develop a happy life in spite of it. In addition to her reinforcement history from past speech therapy, her growing years had been very unhappy. Her father, an alcoholic, had told her repeatedly that her birth was the mistake that ruined his life. She had been born a stutterer to punish her parents for conceiving an unwanted child. Furthermore, because God had created Dorothy as a punishment to others, she would never be able to amount to anything and her life was doomed by God to failure and unhappiness. Her mother, who was terribly afraid of her husband's drunken tirades, finally fled the home with Dorothy and her sisters when they were teenagers. According to her report, Dorothy's first 35 years had been very unhappy ones. She had avoided all social activities, did what was needed to achieve B or C grades in school, and spent most of her time volunteering in religious efforts. She had hoped that by dedicating her life to God and the church she would be able to receive God's forgiveness. According to Dorothy, her friends and colleagues disliked her and gossiped about her. After graduating from high school, she was able to get a full-time church related job and she began to pursue her college education. Although she had successfully completed a graduate training program, she was still experiencing vocational difficulties. She believed that her co-workers continued to dislike her and tried to cause trouble for her that resulted in her decision to move from job to job. However, she believed that her supervisors were able to empathize and understand her feelings and problems, and she began to turn to them for counseling and support. It was in one of these counseling sessions that she was encouraged by her supervisor to enroll in speech therapy as a beginning to resolving her problems generally.

Therapy Schema

During the diagnostic, Dorothy reported that she wanted more than anything in the world to change her speech. She was stuttering 26% of the time and talking at a rate of 107 words per minute. She was rated as having a moderate speech problem by her therapist, but with much more serious social and emotional components. In spite of her feelings that stuttering was her cross to bear, she was very anxious to start therapy. She saw it as the beginning of the end of her problems. During Phase 1, which lasted for three

1-hour sessions, Dorothy stated that she did not feel she needed to be on the DAF machine and that she did not need to slow down her speech. Basically, her pre-therapy speech behavior was characterized by inappropriate pauses in phonation where she felt her throat would not "let the word out." She reported that these blocks occurred about once every 2 or 3 minutes in conversational speech outside the clinic. She did not exhibit repetitions or secondary symptoms; therefore, she saw herself as having only a mild problem that would not require the entire therapy program. After a great deal of discussion, the therapist and Dorothy agreed that it was important and appropriate for her to learn volitional speech control. Nevertheless, during the training she continually increased her rate inappropriately while on the DAF machine and had to be continually reminded to slow down by the therapist. She also experienced marked difficulty learning to produce continuous phonation. She would continually pause inappropriately in the phrase, in a staccato-like fashion. She reported, however, that throughout Phase 1 she did not feel that she ever experienced a stuttering block. In spite of her difficulty, Dorothy completed Phase 1 of therapy after three sessions.

When presented with the Phase II task, self monitoring and self reinforcement, Dorothy again was quick to raise objections. Dorothy's history of preoccupation with her failures and reactions to the evaluations of people in her life suggested that she was a low self-reinforcer who felt as if she were completely controlled by external forces. Primarily, she felt that God alone determined her destiny. She felt that she had no free will or ability to make decisions that might influence the course of her life. As a result, she resisted each part of the self reinforcement paradigm. She did not want to use an overt signal, preferring to think about her speech mentally. She believed that if she consciously monitored her rate and phonation she would increase the probability of blocking. She reasoned that her speech problem was the result of her over-attention to the elements of her motor speech behavior and she would be fluent if somehow she could distract herself from thinking about her speech. Dorothy and the therapist discussed the rationale behind Phase II, emphasizing that if Dorothy programmed a behavior that competed with the undesirable behavior, they could not co-exist. Although she resisted her own success, Dorothy completed Phase II in a 1-hour session with great difficulty. By the end of Phase II, Dorothy was able to monitor stutter-free speech in the clinic very well. She was mildly pleased with her ability to control her speech behavior but felt that at some future time it would completely fall apart.

Gradually we began to develop a contract plan. Because Dorothy was an externally controlled low self-reinforcer we decided to develop an external support system for her. She planned to transfer her speech very slowly with a buddy. Another client agreed to go with her and evaluate her speech while she would evaluate his. During Phase III Dorothy vacillated from feeling good about herself and her speech to intense periods of depression and withdrawal. As soon as she appeared to be doing well, she would actively engage in activities in which she would fail as a speaker and as a person. This was consistently followed by an attack of the flu. During these illnesses she frequently read library books on abnormal psychology that she felt would help her understand her speech problem. By this time, however, she was no longer stuttering in any speaking situation outside the clinic, and was not monitoring. She would occasionally avoid a feared situation. It was almost as if she was full of regret and remorse over her lost stuttering behavior. She would come to therapy, bitterly complaining that she could not have a happy life because of all the terrible things that might happen to her—such as her return to stuttering. She vehemently resisted any reduction in frequency of therapy sessions and continually attempted to encourage the therapist to join her in inappropriate social activities. It appeared that she was trying to arrange her own rejection to confirm that she was not worthy or valued. The therapist tried to keep the focus of their therapy sessions on changing her speech, and as a reaction to a brief discussion about the importance of the therapeutic relationship, Dorothy began to voraciously read books on psychotherapy and the clinical relationship. Dorothy remained in Phase III, Environmental Transfer, for 64 sessions embracing 8½ months. The sessions were gradually decreased from every day to once a month over this period. Dorothy decided that she did not want to go through Phase IV, The Replacement of Monitored Speech with Unmonitored Speech. After 9 months of therapy, she dismissed herself. During her last interview, no stuttering was observed and she was speaking at a rate of 95 words per minute.

Outcome and Impact of Change

Currently, Dorothy has been dismissed from active therapy for 8 months although she contacts her therapist once each month to report on her progress. She states that she is presently no longer stuttering and no longer monitoring her speech. Although she has resigned from her job, she still does volunteer work.

She is now employed in a supervisory capacity for a local business. She still sees herself as a stutterer and still believes that she is in need of some new type of therapy because she does not feel that her speech problem has been completely resolved.

Case 3

The third case study illustrates a slightly different result of therapy. This client no longer stutters, does not view himself as a stutterer, but occasionally monitors his speech under special and infrequent circumstances. His monitoring of speech would be much like the monitoring of a non-stutterer under special talking circumstances and does not include an expectancy to stutter if he does not monitor.

Background Information

Edwin came to the clinic after reading a popular paperback suggesting that stuttering could be cured. Edwin was a very severe stutterer. Several times per minute he would repeat a phoneme over and over with excessive struggling behavior, head jerks, and a glassy stare. He consistently substituted the /p /sound anytime he engaged in his stuttering behavior that had a disastrous effect on the intelligibility of his communication. For example, if he intended to say the word *chair* he would say *p-p-p-pear.* He spoke at a rate of 77 words per minute. His psychological evaluation revealed an extremely high I.Q. on all tests administered. At the time of entering therapy, he was employed part-time as an office assistant. In addition, he worked as a professional free-lance artist and had sold a number of works. He was generally a social isolate and had particular problems with members of his own family. He neither identified with their values nor accepted the high achievement orientation that he perceived in them. He was the black sheep among a group of highly successful and wealthy relatives.

Therapy Schema

Edwin entered therapy eagerly but with great skepticism. He had received several years of psychoanalytic therapy that seemingly had had no effect on his speech or self concept. In fact, he reported that he looked back on the experience with much hostility. In therapy, Edwin stated that he wanted to participate in only the operant conditioning portion of the program and that his inner-thoughts and feelings were no one's business but his own. He completed the first two phases of therapy uneventfully, spending 3 sessions in Phase I and 1½ sessions in Phase II. However, during Phase III he experienced mixed success when speaking on a transfer contract situation. Sometimes he would monitor correctly; other times he would not. The relationship between the client and clinician was not a good one. Edwin saw the clinician as a source of the information he needed to design his own program but tried repeatedly to distance her as much as possible. For example, he would swear at her, call her dirty names, and criticize her personally. During Phase III, it was difficult to help Edwin problem-solve his contract difficulties. He was a high self-reinforcer who insisted that he was going to design his own transfer program, but when he experienced failure he would return to the therapist, enraged that the therapist's program wasn't working. Finally, our consultant on the stuttering project was asked to come to his session to problem-solve the contract activities. The consultant aggressively confronted Edwin with his inappropriate behavior plans, general attitude, and therapy goals. The confrontations were quite aversive and generated a great deal of defensiveness and hostility in Edwin. Both the therapist and Edwin attempted to defend the client's position. After the consultant left, Edwin was very angry and upset while his therapist was empathetic and supportive of his feelings. It was out of this session that Edwin began to trust the therapist and to see her as being committed to his well being. The relationship dynamics began to change and Edwin began to share his feelings with the therapist. He discussed how his self concept and attitudes about himself as a stutterer might be influencing his program in therapy. Edwin reported that he felt as though he had become two people inside one body. Part of him was a stutterer, safe inside the limits of his stuttering personality, avoiding social and vocational endeavors, resenting his unfair plight. The other part of him was a normal speaker, struggling to emerge and succeed. Edwin reported that it seemed as though these two forces were waging war over control of his body. As a result, he often felt physically exhausted and drained. The war continued and the stuttering personality appeared to be dominant. Edwin believed that this part of him intentionally developed schemes to undermine his therapy program. Gradually, however, the new personality began to emerge and grow strong. After 5 months Edwin completed the transfer of his speech response environmentally. Following an additional 3 months he completed the replacement phase, and active therapy was terminated. At the time of termination, Edwin was not stuttering and he was talking at a rate of 185 words per minute. His total therapy for Phase I through IV involved 9 months.

Outcome and Impact of Change

Currently Edwin has been in follow-up for over 1 ½ years. He no longer stutters and sees himself as a normal speaker. He occasionally monitors to practice the feeling of volitional control of his speech mechanism. But generally, he sees the problem as part of his past and does not fear relapse. Edwin believes that his stuttering prevented him from developing socially and vocationally. He had never had a friend or a girl friend and had not confided in his parents or siblings. He feels that he is currently exploring a number of new personal adventures. He talks to co-workers and engages in social activities. He now can relate to the members of his family without feeling apologetic about himself, relating to them with a sense of his own identity and worth both outside and inside his family circle. He is entering into this new world slowly and conservatively but successfully.

In regard to his vocational aspirations, Edwin feels that many career choices are now available to him. At first he was afraid that he had turned to art as a form of expression because he could not talk. Now he feels that regardless of the reason, his art work brings him considerable pleasure and he does not want to abandon it. On the other hand, he is not sure whether being an artist should be a vocation or a hobby and he is exploring other possible careers.

Case 4

The fourth case study is an illustration of a child stutterer who is still in therapy.

Background Information

Joe, a six-year-old boy, came to the clinic presenting a stuttering problem characterized by repetitions, head jerks, and a very rapid rate of speech. Although his overall stuttering frequency was at about 10%, he was rated as having a very severe problem because of the forms of his stuttering behavior. Joe's communicative attempts were often unsuccessful due to the unintelligibility of his speech and his subsequent frustration and withdrawal. He and his parents decided to enroll in therapy as a family.

Therapy Schema

Joe was enrolled in the child stuttering program that met with a group of three other children. He completed training in volitional control of speech in six sessions and training in self reinforcement in two sessions. He then began the third phase of therapy, Environmental Transfer. Joe's mother, father, and younger brother were trained to serve as environmental agents. The home program was designed by the family, and Joe and his brother began to earn points during quiet times at home. Both parents participated in quiet time activities. We expanded contract activity until Joe and his younger brother were using the stutter-free speech response in all communicating interactions at home. At this time both the public school therapist and Joe's classroom teacher were brought into the therapy session. Joe was excited about bringing them to the clinic. He personally wrote letters to each of them explaining his therapy program and why he was inviting them to come to one of his sessions. Joe designed a school program of reinforcement and began contracting at school. At this time, Joe had been receiving therapy over a 4-month period and was doing very well using his new speech in a variety of situations at home and minimally at school.

Outcome and Impact of Change

Gradually Joe began to resist the use of his new speech behavior. He began to use automatic talking characterized by his previous stuttering behavior. He also began to behave very disruptively in group therapy, refusing to participate and demanding chips when he had not produced the correct response. He insisted that he was no longer a stutterer and felt that he was producing stutter-free speech even though he was not.

Currently Joe is also resisting the use of his new speech at home. The parents report that he does not want to participate in home therapy activities and refuses to use his new speech.

To date Joe has been in therapy for 6 months. Within his therapy group, individually, and in the parent group we are attempting to understand Joe's belief system and his reaction to using his new speech. Hopefully, we will be able to develop an appropriate branching step to resolve this problem. Generally, the child stuttering program proceeds rather uneventfully and the child generalizes without ambient difficulty. We chose to include Joe's case history because of its unique problems.

Case 5

The fifth case study is an example of a brief, intensive therapy experience for an adult. She no longer stutters, does not monitor her speech, and does not see herself any longer as a stutterer.

Background Information

Denise, a 27-year-old female, came to the clinic from Mississippi after seeing a news report about the therapy program on television. She enrolled in a 2-week intensive treatment program and received 2 hours of intensive therapy each week day, totaling 20 1-hour therapy sessions. She reported having had a severe stuttering problem since childhood, and although she had received therapy over the years, she had not been able to change her speech behavior. At the time she started therapy she was stuttering 7% of the time she spoke during an initial interview. She was speaking at the rate of 84 words per minute, primarily due to long pauses within and between words.

Therapy Schema

Denise completed the first two phases of therapy, Establishment of Volitional Control of Speech and Training in Self Reinforcement, during the first 4 hours (2 days) of therapy. During the remaining 16 hours (8 days) she designed contract activity, implemented her behavior plans, and evaluated her performance. Although Denise was a high self-reinforcer with an orientation toward internal locus of control, we decided to arrange a buddy system for contract activity. This was not designed to function as a support system, but because Denise was a stranger from out of town, her buddy provided Denise with ample communicative activity for monitoring practice. Denise and another client in intensive therapy spent additional hours together, ordering in restaurants, engaging in heavy discussion, and talking to salespersons. Denise generalized her monitored speech behaviors to her unmonitored speech early during the transfer phase of therapy. She returned to Mississippi after she completed the first three phases of therapy. Upon leaving Denise was not apprehensive about maintaining the new speech behaviors in Mississippi. She had telephoned her family and friends daily during therapy, reporting her processing and demonstrating her new speech response. During a final therapy interview no stuttering was observed in either monitored or unmonitored speech, and her speech rate was 85 words per minute.

Outcome and Impact of Change

Upon her return to Mississippi, Denise maintained her new speaking behavior in all situations. She was so excited about the change in her behavior that she called her local television station to thank the newscaster for informing her of the therapy program. As a result, she appeared on several television programs in Mississippi, describing how she resolved her problem. She reported that these television shows generated a great deal of pressure and tension for her. She stated that she felt this situation was the most difficult speaking situation she would ever attempt. Although she was extremely nervous, she maintained her new speech response correctly. She has continued to speak normally for the past 1½ years. She no longer monitors or sees herself as a stutterer. Currently, she has decided to attend graduate school to become a speech pathologist.

Case 6

Background of Information

This 67-year-old man presented a severe stuttering problem characterized by continual repetitions and blocks. He reported that his speech behavior had interfered with his ability to communicate for the past 60 years and had seriously crippled him professionally and personally. He had been employed as a draftsman during his working years. He had received speech therapy off and on from childhood, and felt that he had not been helped in terms of changing his speech but that he had "gained moral support from concerned therapists." When he began therapy, his stuttering frequency was 8%. He was speaking at a rate of 125 words per minute.

Therapy Schema

Norris completed Phase I, Training in Volitional Control of Speech, after eight 1-hour sessions. He experienced marked difficulty attending to the target behaviors under conditions of DAF, and would constantly speed up his rate and have to be given continuous feedback by the therapist. Furthermore, he would attempt to use other techniques he had learned in previous therapies to avoid stuttering during the Phase I training. Production of these off-target behaviors caused Norris to break down often, and as a result he needed 8 hours rather than the usual 2½ to 3 hours to meet criterion. Once the response was established and he gained volitional control of his speech, he completed the subsequent phases efficiently. Phase II, Training in Self Reinforcement, was completed in 30 minutes; Phase III, Environmental Transfer, was completed in 9½ 1-hour sessions; and Phase IV, Replacement with Unmonitored Speech, was completed in eight sessions. The total time of his therapy program was 26 1-hour sessions over a 6-month period. During his final interview, no stuttering was observed and his speech rate was 177 words per minute.

Outcome and Impact of Change

Norris has been in the follow-up program for the past 9 months. He no longer sees himself as a stutterer; he occasionally monitors in difficult, stressful speaking situations. During his last follow-up evaluation, he produced some subtle off-target behaviors including slight inappropriate pausing and the use of starter type words such as "well um." Norris did not believe that these behaviors were abnormal ones. Although the therapist would judge them to be mild nonfluencies, she felt they were not completely within the realm of normal limits. Norris, however, is convinced that he no longer stutters and is genuinely pleased with the enormous change in his speaking behavior and ability to communicate. Although retired, he has joined several community groups (including a local theatre group) and is taking a public address course. Prior to therapy, he stated that he would have been terrified to engage in such activities.

Case 7

The next case study is not in the typical categories of outcome mentioned earlier. It is a study of a serious relapse and the client's efforts to recapture his earlier success in therapy.

Background Information

Lloyd, age 24, entered therapy with a long history of unsuccessful therapy. He had just received his Master's degree in engineering and was newly and very happily married. He had just landed a job after many interviews that he felt were unsuccessful because of his speech. He was just settling down in a new community.

As an outdoorsman, Lloyd skied, played golf, and drove both a sportscar and motorcycle. He and his wife backpacked in the mountains, thoroughly enjoyed each other, and anticipated a positive future. However, Lloyd's speech was like a black cloud hovering over him; he felt his speech would forever hold him back in his vocation.

When he started therapy, he stuttered about 16% of the time he spoke. His speech was characterized by many interjections and starter phrases, in addition to long pauses or blocks. More than half of his dysfluencies were in the form of total blocks, characterized by extreme muscular tension in the glottal area. He was talking at 154 words per minute.

Lloyd was seen in therapy for 7 months, for a total of 33 visits. When therapy was self-terminated about 2 years ago because he was moving to another city, Lloyd was maintaining fluent speech through use of a reduced speaking rate and continuous phonation. His stuttering frequency was at .3% and his speaking rate was 136 words per minute. As a result of a follow-up study, Lloyd himself initiated the occasion for an additional clinical session, and drove nearly 60 miles roundtrip for his session. He reported that his speech had become progressively more disfluent during the 2 years since he left therapy and especially within the past month. He described his growing difficulty with communication and his gradual withdrawal from the role of an active speaker: "It's all downhill. I don't know what to do." He reported that he was even disfluent when speaking to his dog, a fact that distressed him greatly. He became more willing to let his wife speak for him and he became more dependent on her in almost every social-interactive situation. Lloyd could describe no situation in which he felt confident that he would speak fluently.

Lloyd reported that his growing disfluency was related to his loss of confidence "in what I am trying to do." He identified "trying to keep the hum sound going," "trying to relax," and "avoiding going over the same words and phrases" as behaviors necessary for fluency. These behaviors had become increasingly more difficult for him to maintain.

Although Lloyd had become more and more disfluent over time, he admitted "putting off" doing anything about it. As he described it, his frustration reached a peak recently, and this prompted him to resume therapeutic contact with his therapist. In discussing his delaying contact, Lloyd stated: ". . . it is hard to say something's wrong with you . . . it's like saying you're handicapped . . . but I am . . . quite a bit." At this time his frequency of stuttering had risen to about 14% and his word rate had increased to 155 words per minute.

Lloyd described his speech behavior as having about two disfluencies every minute. Actually, his disfluency rate during the follow-up interview was a good deal higher than that. His underestimation may suggest that he was not "in tune" with his speech behavior. It may also suggest something about the individual's ability to make judgments about his or her own speech behavior.

General Interpretations

When Lloyd started his therapy about 5 years ago, the program of therapy was in its initial developmental stages. Although Phase I, Establishing Volitional Control of Speech, was well established, Phases II, III, and IV did not exist in their present form. The particular problems that Lloyd experienced as a part of his relapse seemed to be directly related to those phases of therapy. Initially, he did not go through those clinical experiences of monitoring, signalling, evaluating, consequating, and replacing that were now available to him at the time of his relapse and his contacting his therapist.

Following his re-evaluation interview, Lloyd was put through an abbreviated DAF program to re-establish a definition of his speech target responses (continuous phonation and slow rate) and a sense of control over his speech. Lloyd met a criterion of 5 minutes at each DAF level instead of 30 minutes as in the basic program. After 30 minutes of progressing through DAF levels of 250 msec., 200, 150, 100, and 50 msec. with stutter-free speech, Lloyd entered Phase II. He learned the elements of Phase II (self reinforcement) and used them with his therapist for 30 minutes. He then began Phase III and started designing therapy contracts. By this time he was also transferring his monitoring behavior to various people in the clinical environment. In 1 ½ hours Lloyd had gone through an abbreviated relapse program, through Phases I and II, and well into Phase III. At that point, because of an impending blizzard and because Lloyd then understood his tasks for Phases III and IV, he left for home. At that time Lloyd was not stuttering with anyone he spoke to in the clinic (students, staff, secretaries, on the telephone). His word rate was down to 101 words per minute and he was continuously monitoring his rate and continuous phonation. He was strongly encouraged by his ability to get back to where he had been in his speech control, and felt much better equipped and motivated to pursue his therapy on his own. For a period of 6 months, Lloyd contacted his therapist at first on a weekly basis and then on a monthly basis. Each night he would tape record a review of his contract activities and mail the cassette to his therapist for his review and evaluation. These long distance contacts revealed an initial surge of enthusiasm and success, followed by a period of relatively little progress and considerable discouragement. Lloyd again felt he was being deceived by the coincidental fluency that often accompanies monitoring. He felt that he didn't need to monitor his speech and started to drift away from monitoring. Plans were made for another visit to the clinic when he started to observe an increase in stuttering behavior. However, this time he recognized his problems and promptly started to do something about them. He increased his monitoring activities and made them more systematic. Plans for the clinic visit were dropped and Lloyd continued with his cassette contact, showing a steady, systematic, and progressive expansion of contract activity. Of equal importance was Lloyd's developing abilities to see and correct his problems on his own, and an understanding of what he had to do to reach his goals.

Chapter 9

Comments on the Public School Setting

Introduction

The professional context in which each of us works organizes the opportunity and the physical arrangements that provide our services to our clients. As such, each of these working contexts, whether it be a hospital setting, a rehabilitation center or a public or private school situation functions within a larger perspective of a specific agency. Their respective operating procedures, rules, regulations, policies, philosophies, and personalities are attributes that are facilitative, designed to provide the best possible service to the person with a problem. However, sometimes agencies operate under constraints that can limit professional productiveness and effectiveness. These constraints obviously vary from agency to agency. The degree of their impact on our effectiveness appears to be a function of their nature, the motivation of the client to push ahead in spite of them, and the willingness and ingenuity of the clinician to either circumvent or reduce their impact. However, one axiom should guide us: "You must have contact with your client (see her) if you are going to help her."

The motivated client and the concerned and caring clinician can do wonders, even in the boiler room of a school or in the corridor of a hospital. Although these latter types of working conditions have become a part of our legend or mythology, in some cases they do exist, symbolically if not literally, as constraints on our ability to help.

We will especially examine some of the agency constraints that could be factors in successfully carrying out this particular therapy for stuttering, and we will suggest ways for resolving these issues. We will particularly focus on the public school context, primarily because most questions we have received at workshops and in the mail about these issues have been from public school speech therapists. We will approach our discussion by exploring the various phases of the therapy, revealing specific constraining issues, and finally, suggesting procedures that have been effective for neutralizing constraints.

When we look at the activities of Phase I, designed to establish volitional control of speaking that results in monitored fluency, two issues are paramount. One is the usefulness of expensive equipment in the form of a delayed auditory feedback recorder; the other is the initially brief intensive schedule of therapy.

Equipment

Many agencies, including schools, cannot afford expensive equipment for large scale or perhaps even small scale use. Limited funds can preclude such purchases. Although the use of the DAF machine has proven to be effective in Phase I of this therapy, it is not essential. This therapy is not exclusively DAF therapy and it would be unfortunate if the many other parameters and attributes of this therapy were lost or forgotten, possibly because of the dramatic changes associated with the use of the DAF machine in Phase I.

Especially with very young children, we have found that having the client imitate the rate and continuous phonation models provided by the clinician is preferable to using the DAF machine. Such devices as hand puppets, specific locations (a slow-speech chair and a fast-speech chair), and electronically-voice controlled moving dolls have been effectively used to establish volitional control of speech with children. It is also possible to use audiotapes that contain samples of various rates of talking (with continuous phonation) for the same kind of training. These tapes are available through this publisher or can be self-made. They are organized so that a particular rate of talking associated with each of the five DAF levels is heard on an audiotape and the client is reinforced for imitating the sample. Eventually, the clinician's model or the tape recorded model is faded out, and the client produces the appropriate rate independently under the same time criteria employed with the DAF machine. Once Phase I is completed in this manner, the stutterer moves into Phase II in a manner similar to those clients who had used a DAF machine.

It should be remembered that for children, Phase I (with a DAF machine) usually takes about 5 hours to complete. These 5 hours involve using the criterion of 15 minutes per child at each of the five delay-speech rate intervals. Each child accumulates a total of 75 minutes of talking time at five specifically controlled speech rates. With four children in the group the total time equals 5 hours for the group with or without a DAF machine. After that, the DAF machine or clinician examples are no longer a formal part of the therapy.

In some instances, a school district can purchase only one DAF machine to be shared. Under these circumstances the DAF machine can be rotated among therapists since it is used for such a short time with any one specific stutterer or group of stutterers. Thus, one machine can serve a large number of stutterers with appropriate scheduling and planning of these 5-hour blocks of time.

The Schedule

The issue of the initially brief intensive schedule is not so easily resolved. In Phase I and II, the intensive daily schedule seems to be imperative. On a less intensive therapy schedule, we have found that time in each session must be spent in reviewing the activities of the previous session in order to re-establish the target responses. A non-intensive schedule is like taking two steps forward and one step backward; it prolongs Phase I quite significantly. Under such circumstances the stutterer perceives the initial changes in speech as less profound, the intensity of the therapy regime is diminished, and the stutterer's motivation and enthusiasm suffers. Ideally, the daily schedule should be sustained for two weeks as the client is well into Phase III transfer activities. However, after five to six days to complete Phases I and II, the daily schedule can be reduced if necessary, but only after the client is well into Phase III. Although this early reduction in the schedule is less than ideal, if the client is highly motivated and has easily learned the Phase II tactics of self regulation, a reduction in the therapy schedule will not jeopardize success. The clinician should see the client at least twice a week, if at all possible, until he is confident that the client is steadily progressing through her Phase III strategies. Usually within four to five weeks the sessions can be reduced to once a week; within eight weeks the client may be seen once a month as she enters her replacement of monitoring and follow-up stages of therapy.

Obviously, as the schedule for one group of stutterers is being reduced, another group may be started on an intensive basis. Children with other types of communication problems can be inserted into the vacated time slots on a non-intensive basis if that is so desired. In this way, a balance can be maintained between intensively scheduled stutterers and non-intensively scheduled clients who have other problems.

If a school therapist is on a time-block schedule whereby service is provided to a particular school on an intensive basis for perhaps a month at a time, the schedule is then much less of a problem. Following that initial month of intensive service, transfer and follow-up schedules can be handled more flexibly in very short periods of contact later. If the child is still in Phase III transfer activities after the first month, then other assistance should be mobilized. Parents, teachers, peers, and older children in the school can be of assistance.

The intially intensive schedule of this therapy should not be compromised, and all ways to preserve this aspect of the program should be exhausted. If it is not at all possible for the therapist to see a stutterer intensively, then a collaborative effort should be arranged whereby the public school therapist can refer the stutterer for the initially intensive phases of therapy to an agency where such programming can be arranged. It may be possible to designate one person in the school system who will have the responsibility for the brief and intensive experiences of Phase I and Phase II, perhaps on an itinerary basis. If the person is not within the school system, then a person can be used from an agency outside the school system. Once the stutterer progresses through these phases she can be referred again to her regular speech therapist for the remainder of her therapy. Later, the school therapist can become active on a less intensive basis during transfer and follow-up activities. Such collaborations have in fact been arranged in a number of cases and have worked quite well when communication among all those involved has been open and frequent. The success in such collaborations seems to depend on having the public school therapist and the agency that carries on the intensive work be involved with each other from the beginning. Success also depends on the maintenance of functional contact throughout so that each party understands his respective role in the overall program of therapy.

The Parents

In the child program format described earlier in the book, parent training is required if it is at all possible. For the pre-school child, the parent is primarily responsible for transfer opportunity of the Phase III tactics. However, it may be quite difficult to bring parents into the school situation and train them in those transfer and reinforcement tactics previously described in the non-school setting. Fortunately, by the time the child reaches school age, she spends nearly as much time at school as she does at home. Therefore, a classroom teacher, a peer, or an older student could be used as a parent substitute for initial transfer activities. The child, the therapist, and the parent substitute could then design "contract" activities that utilize situations and people found at school. Once the monitoring activities are strongly established at school, the home transfer program can be initiated. This arrangement is the opposite of the program for the non-school setting described in Chapter 6. In those non-school settings, the parent usually brings the child into the clinic and is therefore available for the parent-training program. In the school setting, the child typically is left at the school for the school day while the parent goes about his daily routines away from school. Actually, support systems for transferring the child's monitoring both at home and at school should be arranged. The sequence of the development of these support systems may vary with the individual circumstances and motivations of each child, of her parents, and of her teachers.

The provision of therapy for stuttering in the schools is not necessarily long-term nor complicated. With appropriate planning, scheduling, and involvement with parents, teachers, and other pupils, such therapy in the schools can be quite as effectively carried out as in non-school settings.

Bibliography

Andrews, G. Editorial: Token reinforcement systems. *Australian and New Zealand Journal of Psychiatry*, 1971, *5*, 135–136.

Bellack, A., Rozensky, R., and Schwartz, J. *Self monitoring as an adjunct to a behavioral weight reduction program.* Paper presented at APA Convention, 1973

Bellack, A.S., and Tillman, W. Effects of tasks and experimenter feedback on the self-reinforcement behavior of internals and externals. *Journal of Consulting and Clinical Psychology*, 1974, *42*, 330–36

Blind, J., Egolf, D., and Shames, G. *Critical factors for the carryover of fluency in stutterers.* Paper presented at American Speech and Hearing Assoc. Convention, San Francisco, 1972.

Brookshire, R.H., and Eveslage, R. Verbal punishment of disfluency following augmentation of random delivery of aversive stimuli. *Journal of Speech and Hearing Research*, 1969, *42*, 383–388

Curlee, R.F., and Perkins, W.H. Conversational rate control therapy for stuttering. *Journal of Speech and Hearing Disorders*, 1969, *34*, 245–250.

Derisi, W.J., and Butz, G. *Writing Behavioral Contracts, a Case Simulation Manual.* Champaign, Illinois: Research Press, 1975.

Flanagan, B., Goldiamond, I., and Azrin, N.H. Operant stuttering: The control of stuttering behavior through response contingent consequences. *Journal of Experimental Analysis of Behavior*, 1958, *1*, 173–177.

Glick, I.J., and Kessler, D.R. *Marital and family therapy,* New York: Grune and Stratton, Inc., 1974.

Haan, N. *Coping and defending processes of self-environment organization,* New York: Academic Press, 1977.

Halvorson, J. The effects on stuttering frequency of pairing punishment (response cost) with reinforcement. *Journal of Speech and Hearing Research*, 1971, *14*, 356–364.

Honeygosky, R. *The conditioning of verbal expressions of anger.* Unpublished research project, University of Pittsburgh, 1966.

Ingham, R., and Andrews, G. Behavior therapy and stuttering: A review. *Journal of Speech and Hearing Disorders*, (1973), *38*, 405–411.

Ingham, R., and Andrews, G., Stuttering: The quality of fluency after treatment. *Journal of Communication Disorders*, 1971, *4*, 279–288.

Ingham, R., Andrews, G., and Winkler, R. Stuttering: A comparative evaluation of the short-term effectiveness of four treatment techniques. *Journal of Communication Disorders*, 1972, *5*, 91–117.

Ivey, A. Microcounseling, *Innovations in interviewing training,* Springfield, Illinois: Charles C. Thomas, 1976.

Johnson, C. *Verbal conditioning of a stutterer in a therapeutic context.* Master's thesis, University of Pittsburgh, 1966.

Kanfer, F. The many faces of self control or behavior modification changes its focus. In Richard Stuart (Ed.), *Behavioral self management strategies, technique and outcome.* (New York: Brunner/Mazel Publishers, 1974.

Kanfer, F., and Karoly, P. Self-control: A behavioristic excursion into the lion's den. *Behavior Therapy*, 1972, *3*, 398–416.

Kasprisin-Burrelli, A., Egolf, D.B., and Shames, G.H. A comparison of parental verbal behavior with stuttering and nonstuttering children. *Journal of Communication Disorders,* 1972, 5, 335-346.

Kodish, M., and Tucciarone, M. *Increasing the average fluency interval: An individualized operant conditioning therapy program.* Unpublished research, University of Pittsburgh, 1973.

Kolb, D., Winter, S., and Berlew, D. Self-directed change: Two studies. *Journal of Applied Behavioral Science,* 1968, *4,* 453-471.

Lathman, S.G., and Kirschenbaum, M. *The dynamic family,* Palo Alto, California: Science and Behavior Books, Inc., 1974.

Leach, E. Stuttering: Clinical application of response contingent procedures. In B. Gray & E. England (Eds.), *Stuttering and the conditioning therapies,* Monterey, California: Monterey Institute for Speech and Hearing, 1969.

Lefcourt, H. Internal vs. external control of reinforcement: A review. *Psychological Bulletin,* 1966, *65,* 206-220.

Leith, W.R., and Uhlemann, M.R. *The shaping group: Theory, organizaton and function.* Scientific Exhibit at American Speech and Hearing Association Convention, 1970a.

Leith, W.R., and Uhlemann, M.R., *The shaping group approach to stuttering. A clinical investigation.* Scientific Exhibit at American Speech and Hearing Association Convention, 1970b.

Leith, W.R., and Uhlemann, M.R. *The treatment of stuttering by the shaping group.* Paper presented at American Speech and Hearing Association Convention, 1970c.

Locke, S., Cartledge, N., and Koeppel, J. Motivational effect of knowledge of results: A goal setting phenomenon? *Psychological Bulletin,* 1968, *70,* 474-485.

Mahoney, M.J. Research issues in self-management. *Behavioral Therapy,* 1972a, *3,* 145-63.

Mahoney, M.J., Mowra, N.G.M., and Wade, T.C. The relative efficacy of self-reward, self punishment and self monitoring techniques for weight loss. *Journal of Consulting And Clinical Psychology,* 1973, *40,* 404-410.

Marston, A. Self-reinforcement: The relevance of a concept in analogue research to psychotherapy. *Psychotherapy: Theory, Research And Practice,* 1965, *2,* 1-5.

Martin, R.R., and Ingham, R.J. Stuttering. In B. Lahey (ed.), *The modification of language behavior.* Springfield, Ill.: Charles C. Thomas, 1973.

Martin, R.R., and Siegel, G.M. The effects of response contingent shock on stuttering. *Journal of Speech and Hearing Research,* 1966a, *9,* 340-52.

McFall, R., Effects of self-monitoring on normal smoking behavior. *Journal of Consulting and Clinical Psychology,* 1970, *35,* 135-142.

McFall, R., and Hammen, C., Motivation, structure and self-monitoring: role of non-specific factors in smoking reduction. *Journal of Consulting and Clinical Psychology,* 1971, *37,* 80-86.

Perkins, W.H. *Speech pathology: An applied behavioral science.* St. Louis, Missouri: C.V. Mosby, 1971.

Perkins, W.H. Replacement of stuttering with normal speech: I. rationale. *Journal of Speech And Hearing Disorders,* 1973a, *38,* 283-294.

Perkins, W.H. Replacement of stuttering with normal speech: II. Clinical procedures. *Journal of Speech And Hearing Disorders,* 1973b, *38,* 295-303.

Premack, D., Toward empirical behavior laws: 1. positive reinforcement. *Psychology Review,* 1959, *66,* 219-233.

Rickard, H., and Mundy, M. Direct manipulation of stuttering behavior: An experimental and clinical approach. In L. Ullmann and L. Krasner (Eds.), Case studies in behavior modification. New York: Holt, Rinehart and Winston, 1965.

Rogers, C. *Patterns of Processes that Take Place in Encounter Groups,* Information Cassette Series. Chicago: Instructional Dynamics, Inc., 1972.

Rogers, C. and Dymond, R. (Eds.) *Psychotherapy and personality change,* Chicago: University of Chicago Press, 1954.

Rogers, C. *Counseling and psychotherapy,* Cambridge, Mass.: Houghton-Mifflin, 1942.

Rotter, J. Generalized expectancies for internal versus external control of reinforcement. *Psychological Monographs,* 1966, *80*, (1, whole No. 609).

Rozensky, R.H. *The manipulation of temporal placement of self monitoring: A case study of smoking reduction.* Unpublished paper, 1973.

Rozensky, R.H. *The tendency to self-reinforce as a diagnostic and predictor variable for success in self versus externally controlled therapeutic programs for weight reduction.* Doctoral dissertation, University of Pittsburgh, 1974.

Ryan, B. Operant procedures applied to stuttering therapy for children. *Journal of Speech and Hearing Disorders,* 1971, *36*, 264–280.

Ryan, B., and Van Kirk, B. The establishment, transfer and maintenance of fluent speech in 50 stutterers using delayed auditory feedback and operant procedures. *Journal of Speech and Hearing Disorders,* 1974, *39*, 3–10.

Schmidt, Jerry A., *Help yourself, a guide to self-change,* Champaign, Ill.: Research Press, 1976.

Shames, G.H., and Egolf, D.B. *Operant conditioning and the management of stuttering; A book for clinicians,* Englewood Cliffs, New Jersey: Prentice-Hall, Inc., 1976.

Shames, G.H., and Florance, C.L. *Behavioral Management of Stuttering.* Short course at National Convention of ASHA, Chicago, 1977.

Shames, G.H., Egolf, D.B., and Rhodes, R.C. Experimental programs in stuttering therapy. *Journal of Speech and Hearing Disorders,* 1969, *34*, 30–47.

Shames, G.H., and Sherrick, C.E., Jr. A discussion of nonfluency and stuttering as operant behavior. *Journal of Speech and Hearing Disorders,* 1963, *28*, 3–18.

Shaw, C., and Shrum, W. The effects of response-contingent reward on the connected speech of children who stutter. *Journal of Speech and Hearing Disorders,* 1972, *37*, 75–88.

Siegel, G.M. Punishment, stuttering and disfluency. *Journal of Speech and Hearing Research,* 1970, *13*, 677–714.

Skinner, B.F. *Science and human behavior.* New York: MacMillan, 1953.

Strupp, H., Patient-Doctor Relationship: Psychotherapist in the Therapeutic Process in H.J. Bachrach (Ed.) *Experimental foundations of clinical psychology,* New York: Basic Books, 1962.

Strupp, H. On the Technology of Psychotherapy. *Archives of General Psychiatry,* 1972, *26*, 270–278.

Van Riper, C. *The treatment of stuttering.* Englewood Cliffs, New Jersey: Prentice-Hall, 1973.

Witzel, M.A., and Schulman, E. *The effect of a response-cost paradigm on the length of a stutterer's fluency interval.* Unpublished research, University of Pittsburgh, 1973.

Appendix

Parent-Child Interaction Analysis*

A method for assessing parent-child interaction patterns has been constructed. Assessment is made by observing parent-child interactions and categorizing each statement that the parent makes into one of 17 positive categories or one of 18 negative categories (see attachments). Positive statements lead to mutual understanding and trust while negative statements are those that lead to misunderstanding, distrust, hostility and aggression.

The method is derived from the content of *Between Parent and Child* by Haim Ginott and from our own experience. Pervading the method overall are the two basic suggestions of Ginott: (1) Statements of understanding should precede statements of advice and instruction, and (2) Both the parent and the child have personalities that must be respected.

---

* Kaspirsin-Burrelli, A., Egolf, D.G., and Shames, G., A Comparison of Parental Verbal Behavior with Stuttering and Nonstuttering Children. *J. Comm. Dis.*, 5, 1972, 335–346.

Positive Language Categories

1. *Positive Questions:* positive questions are those which encourage vocalization; e.g., "What did you do in school today".

2. *Positive Advice:* advice which is preceded by understanding; e.g., "IF you are well rested you are stronger. That's why you should go to bed early."

3. *Positive Praise:* praise aimed at the child's actions or deeds instead of his personality; e.g., "You did a fine job washing the car."

4. *Positive Comparison:* a comparison that indicates understanding; e.g., "Sometimes even I am afraid of the dark".

5. *Event-Feeling:* a statement which takes into account the feeling of the child when he relates an event; e.g., if the child says that the teacher yelled at him in school, a good event-feeling statement would be, "I guess you were quite embarrassed."

6. *Sequitur:* any statement which follows content-wise the direction of the child's conversation.

7. *Positive Criticism:* criticism which is preceded by understanding; e.g., "I know you are restless but you can't pull the curtain in the clinic."

8. *Verbal-Lubricant:* any utterance which demonstrates attentiveness and interest on the part of the listener; e.g., "That's interesting—tell me more."

9. *Mirrors-Personality:* a statement which reflects the child's apparent feelings, e.g., "I see you are angry now."

10. *Permits ambivalence:* a statement which shows acceptance of bipolar feelings; e.g., "Sometimes you just don't like your brother."

11. *Identifies Reasons for Emotions:* a statement which helps the child localize the focus of his emotions; e.g., "It looks like you might be kicking things around because your brother got a letter today and you didn't."

12. *Understands Feelings:* a statement which helps the child accept a feeling; e.g., "I know you would like to receive a letter too."

13. *Humor:* common laughter without any trace of sarcasm.

14. *Qualifying:* statements preceded by "If, I think, I guess."

15. *Information:* any statement which presents new information; e.g., "While you were at school, grandma called."

16. *Parent's Thoughts and Feelings:* any statement that shows the parent identifying this thoughts and feelings and the reasons for them.

17. *Other:* a residual category made available to place any positive statement that does not fit easily into any of the above positive categories.

Negative Language Categories

1. *Negative Questions:* questions that cause the child to lie, that can be answered by a yes or no, or that have obvious answers; e.g., "Do you like your teacher?"
2. *Negative Advice:* advice not preceded by understanding.
3. *Negative Praise:* praise that is global and not directed to a specific act; e.g., "You're just such a good boy."
4. *Negative Comparison:* comparison which attacks the personality; e.g., "Your brother never had a "D" in spelling."
5. *Event-Feeling:* a statement which shows a reaction to an event when a feeling should be reacted to; e.g., if the child says he was "Yelled at" in school, a negative response would be, "You must have been bad."
6. *Non-Sequitur:* self-explanatory.
7. *Negative Criticism:* criticism not preceded by understanding.
8. *Insults:* self-explanatory.
9. *Sarcasm:* Self-explanatory
10. *Prophesying:* a statement which makes a dire prediction; e.g., "If you keep rubbing your eyes, you will go blind."
11. *Threats:* "If you don't shut-up you're going to get it when we get home."
12. *Bribes:* "If you are good, we'll stop at the store."
13. *Dictates Feelings:* statements which tell the child how to feel; e.g., "You should be happy."
14. *Dictates Actions:* statements which direct child's behavior; e.g,. "Look at the man when you talk."
15. *Denials:* statements wherein the parent denies something without explanation; e.g., "Your father wasn't mad at you."
16. *Aborts:* statements which seemingly show acceptance but by their manner disrupt conversation; e.g., "That's very interesting but now I want to tell you something."
17. *Interruptions:* self-explanatory.
18. *Other:* a residual category made available to place any negative statement that does not fit easily into any of the above negative categories.

I.D. _____
Name _____
Date _____
Session No. _____
Page ____ of ____

Interrogation Rating   1 2 3 4 5 6 7
Emotional Tone   1 2 3 4 5 6 7
Equilibrium   1 2 3 4 5 6 7
_____
_____

POSITIVE
1. Good Questions
2. Good Advice
3. Good Praise
4. Good Comparison
5. Event–Feeling
6. Sequitur
7. Good Criticism
8. Verbal Lubricant
9. Mirrors Personality
10. Permits Ambivalence
11. Id. Rsns. for Emot.
12. Understands Feelings
13. Humor
14. Qualifying
15. Information
16. P.'s thogt. & Feels.
17. Other

NEGATIVE
1. Bad Questions
2. Bad Advice
3. Bad Praise
4. Bad Comparison
5. Event–Feeling
6. Non-Sequitur
7. Bad Criticism
8. Insults
9. Sarcasm
10. Prophesying
11. Threats
12. Bribes
13. Dictates Feels.
14. Dictates Actions
15. Denials
16. Aborts
17. Interruptions

168

Index